GETTING GOOD GRADES

Marjorie Ewing Aghassi is Associate Professor of Political Science and Pre-Law Advisor at New College of Hofstra University. Originally from Chicago, she received her BA degree from the University of Chicago, her MA and PhD degrees from Columbia University. She has worked in the field of personnel management and written a pamphlet on the assessment of personnel management techniques for the United States Civil Service Commission. From time to time, she has constructed test items in social science for the American College Testing Program.

GETTING GOOD GRADES
How to Succeed in College

378
AGH

MARJORIE EWING AGHASSI

A SPECTRUM BOOK

PRENTICE-HALL, INC., *Englewood Cliffs, New Jersey 07632*

11292

Library of Congress Cataloging in Publication Data

Aghassi, Marjorie Ewing.
  Getting good grades.

  (A Spectrum Book)
  Includes index.
  1. Study, Method of—Handbooks, manuals, etc.
2. College student orientation—Handbooks,
manuals, etc.   I. Title.
LB2395.A34   378′.1702812   79–28578
ISBN 0–13–354514–8
ISBN 0–13–354506–7 pbk.

X III, 144p illus

Design and production by Kingsport Press Editorial & Graphic Services
Kingsport, Tennessee 37662

ⓒ 1980 by Prentice-Hall, Inc., Englewood Cliffs, New Jersey 07632

A SPECTRUM BOOK

10   9   8   7   6   5   4   3   2   1

Printed in the United States of America

PRENTICE-HALL INTERNATIONAL, INC., *London*
PRENTICE-HALL OF AUSTRALIA PTY. LIMITED, *Sydney*
PRENTICE-HALL OF CANADA, LTD., *Toronto*
PRENTICE-HALL OF INDIA PRIVATE LIMITED, *New Delhi*
PRENTICE-HALL OF JAPAN, INC., *Tokyo*
PRENTICE-HALL OF SOUTHEAST ASIA PTE. LTD., *Singapore*
WHITEHALL BOOKS LIMITED, *Wellington, New Zealand*

Courtesy of Vic Cantone

Contents

Preface xii

I. *Getting Good Grades: A Skill to Be Learned* 1
The Importance of Good Grades 1
A Skill to Be Learned 2
How this Book Can Help You 2

II. *Planning for Career and College* 4
Knowing Yourself 4
Choosing a Tentative Career 7
Selecting a College 9
Selecting a Major 12

III. *Planning Your Semester's Work* 14
Planning Semester Course Load 15
Planning Your Study Load
to Keep Up Your GPA 16
Keeping Yourself Working 21
The Advantages of Planning 22

IV. *Using Study Time Effectively* 23
Allowing Enough Time for Study   23
Using Available Time Appropriately   24
Concentrating on the Task at Hand   26
Using Your Non-Conscious Mind   30
Using Concentration   30
Making the Use of Study Time Rewarding   31

V. *Reading for College Courses* 32
Structure of a Textbook   32
Remembering What the Book Says   38
Improving Your Reading   47
Advantages of Being a Good Reader   47

VI. *Getting the Most Out of Classes* 49
Going to Class Pays Off   49
Using Class Time Effectively   51

VII. *Writing Research Papers* 57
Make It Your Own   57
Picking a Topic   58
Planning How to Write About Your Topic   60
Doing Research   63
Writing Your Paper   69
Some General Suggestions   72
The Value of Writing Papers   73

VIII. *Studying for Examinations* 74
Learning What You Can in Advance   75
Reviewing for Objective Examinations   81
Reviewing for Essay Examinations   82
Getting Some Rest Before the Examination   83

IX. *Taking Examinations* 84
Answering Objective Questions   85
Answering Essay Questions   90

Rereading the Finished Examination 100
Reviewing the Graded Examination 100

X. ***After College, Where?*** **102**
More School or a Job? 103
Getting into Graduate or Professional School 105
Finding a Decent Job 111

Appendix A ***Tools of the Student*** **121**
Dictionary 121
Grammar Book 122
Personal File 122
College Bulletins 123
Typewriter 124

Appendix B ***Using the College
  Library*** **125**
Parts of the College Library 125
Getting Help from the Librarians 136

PREFACE

Getting Good Grades: How to Succeed in College is written for any student who wants to do his or her best academically. Although it is addressed primarily to the young person about to enter a four-year college, other students will also find its guidance valuable.

Indeed, the student who comes into a bachelor's program at the junior year may be the person with the greatest need for the book. Experience shows that one of the most difficult educational transitions is from a junior or community college to a four-year college. The gap between a junior college graduate and his or her peer at the third year of a bachelor's degree program is usually much greater than it was when both graduated from high school. This book can help the young person who hopes to get as good grades after his or her transfer to a Bachelor of Arts program as he or she did in the Associate of Arts program.

Another student who can benefit from this book—and who may be the first to reach for it—is the adult who is returning to school after years away. Unlike the person coming in from a community college, this person is often painfully aware of deficiencies in educational background. He or she may even exaggerate them, may feel inferior to the recent high school graduate and may fear exposing his or her ignorance. It is true that these returnees to the educational world are often those who greatly undervalued education in their high school years and hence never learned the skills and discipline necessary for successful study. However, these students are often the most highly motivated and thus the best able to learn what this book has to teach.

Also, it is hoped that juniors and seniors in high school will take advantage of this book, for they are in the best position to benefit from it. Finally, any student, regardless of educational level, who feels he ought to get better grades than he is getting can learn improved methods of study from this book.

Getting Good Grades is concerned with those problems shown by eighteen years of teaching and student advisement experience to be the major weaknesses of incoming college students. These are lack of self-awareness respecting those skills and traits that count in college, inability to plan college work so as to get it done and lack of self-discipline to do it, and inadequate reading, writing, and study skills. Unfortunately, the student who comes to college with such educational gaps usually leaves with them, too, unless he or she makes a strong effort to overcome them. This book is designed to help any student who is weak in these areas to learn what the problems are and how to overcome them.

If you are not getting the grades you think you should be able to get, this book is for you. Conversely, if you are afraid to take on a further educational experience because you fear exposing your ignorance, it is for you, too.

Because this book has grown out of observation of students and the ways they and their teachers have tackled these problems, I want to express my gratitude to my students and to my colleagues, especially those at New College of Hofstra University, for much that is in it.

GETTING GOOD GRADES

CHAPTER I

Getting Good Grades: A Skill to be Learned

This book is written for the student who wants to get good grades in college. Of course, there are many good things to be gotten from going to college besides good grades. However, this book is addressed only to the problem of your scholastic record, because no matter what else you get out of college unless your grades are good, you have to some extent failed yourself.

THE IMPORTANCE OF GOOD GRADES

Good grades are important for two reasons. First, they determine your educational progress. They are a measure—a rough one to be sure, but nonetheless a measure—of your past learning and your past diligence. Therefore, admission to higher levels of education—graduate school, professional school—is based very much on your grades in college. Some schools believe that class standing, which is determined by comparing your grades with those of your classmates, is the best predictor of your success in graduate or professional school. And in some fields it is also a good predictor of success in your profession as well. Therefore, schools and employers, even those that depend primarily on tests to estimate an applicant's chances of success, give great weight to an applicant's grades.

Second, grades are frequently a basis for one's estimate of oneself. In a society in which credentials, including grades, are important for getting ahead and in which success is a mark of worth, it is almost inevitable that a person should judge him- or herself according to the grades that teachers have assigned to him or her. Thus, if your grades are low, your self-esteem is likely to be low, too. Therefore, it should be encouraging to read that you can *learn* how to get better grades.

A SKILL TO BE LEARNED

Getting good grades is not just a matter of the intelligence a person is born with. In fact, even though we have IQ tests that are supposed to measure "native" intelligence, we know that if we change the circumstances under which people live, their intelligence will change, too. So we know that to some extent people learn to be intelligent.

We know also that regular study is an important part of getting good grades. Because regular study is a habit, it too can be learned. Changing old habits is not easy, but it is possible, and there are ways to make it easier. If you wanted to learn to ice skate or to play tennis, you would get someone to show you the right way, and then you would practice. That is what this book is for—to show you the right way.

HOW THIS BOOK CAN
HELP YOU

Many things contribute to the grades you get. Choosing the right course of study and the right college are the first steps. These take proper planning. Chapter II tells you how to go about this kind of planning.

Planning can also be used to balance your work load and to motivate you to work regularly. Chapter III is devoted to this kind of planning.

Many students do not use well the time they have for study. Chapter IV shows you ways to use your time better.

Reading to understand and remember is the most important single skill a student can have. Chapter V discusses the way you can improve your reading of the most common types of college reading materials.

Going to class is not simply a matter of being physically present in the classroom. Chapter VI shows you how to use your class time to your best advantage.

The papers you write usually contribute significantly to your grade, and writing papers is an important skill in itself. Chapter VII discusses how to write the most common type of college paper.

Examination grades are usually the biggest part of your final grade in any course. Chapters VIII and IX explain how best to review for and take examinations.

Chapter X examines post-college opportunities. It discusses particularly whether or not to go on for more advanced education or to look for work.

Two appendixes at the end of this book can help you to make the best use of the common tools of the student and of that valuable resource, the college library.

Here are the means to achieve some of what you are going to college for. Don't just read this book; work with it. Whenever you undertake to do a particular-type task, consult that chapter which is devoted to the best way to accomplish it. Through practicing the techniques described, you will eventually develop habits that will make studying easier. Learning is work, of course, and always will be. However, for those who do it well and earn its rewards, learning is pleasurable and satisfying work. May it become so for you.

CHAPTER II

Planning
for Career and College

Planning is the first key to success. You should start by planning a tentative career and selecting an appropriate college. The career you think about now may not be the one you will end up with. But planning in the expectation of a career will make you think about where you are going and about your own interests, abilities, and weaknesses. Good planning requires information not only about schools, curricula, and courses but, first of all, about yourself.

KNOWING YOURSELF

Many students know very little about themselves, at least about those aspects of themselves that are important to success in college. Lack of self-awareness has many causes. Self-assessment by students often reflects society's view of what is appropriate for their sex. Young women frequently say that they are no good at math or science simply because they have heard that women do not do well at mathematics and science. Boys sometimes avoid dance or art because those fields are seen as sissy. Some students underestimate their abilities because they recall an early weakness that they do not realize they have overcome. A boy who has had a reading problem in the early years of school may go on thinking of himself as a poor reader after he has caught up. On the other hand, because it is natural to hide weaknesses even

4

from ourselves, some students are unaware that they have them. For example, a distaste for writing papers may be the outcome of a poor use of English, a weakness that can be remedied only if the student will admit he has it. Finally, students often reflect uncritically the views of relatives or friends. Some students are convinced that they won't like or can't do accounting or statistics or psychology or some other field of study because a friend or relative has said that he or she didn't like it or couldn't do it. Poorly founded impressions of oneself are often believed firmly and can be the cause of very poor educational planning.

Collect Objective Data

You should collect as much objective information about yourself as you can. Assemble a file of your school report cards; get from your high school whatever records and teacher comments are available. Ask for your class ranking, which is often given in deciles. The first decile is the highest; the ninth is the lowest.[1] If your school has given IQ (intelligence quotient) tests, aptitude tests, or vocational preference tests, request a copy of your scores.[2] If you do not understand what they mean, ask your guidance counselor or the school psychologist to explain them.

The results of any special testing program you may have undertaken should be included. If you are already in college, you can request your college's counseling office to give you such tests as they offer. These tests are frequently offered free to students who are paying full tuition.

Many college-bound students take the College Entrance Examinations (Scholastic Aptitude Test's) or the American College Testing Services examinations (ACT's). The SAT now includes three scores—a Verbal, a Mathematical, and an English (Test of Standard Written English or TSWE). The Math and Verbal scores are given in three figures (for example, 545) and the TSWE score

---

[1] Colleges frequently state their admission standards partially in terms of decile ranking.

[2] You are entitled to these by law.

is in two figures (for example, 42). SAT scores show you whether your greater ability is verbal or mathematical and how you compare with others who have taken these examinations. The average score in either Math or Verbal is 500. About two-thirds of all students taking the exam have scores between 400 and 600; about 95 percent are between 300 and 700. So, if you have a score of 610, you are in the upper one-sixth of those who have taken the test. The highest TSWE score is 60+, and experience shows that a person who gets a score of 50 or better can write satisfactory English.

The report of your examination will also give your percentile rank. This is similar to the decile rank in your graduating class, but there are two differences. Percentiles divide all the test scores into ninety-nine (instead of nine) parts, and in reporting percentiles, the first is the lowest (instead of the highest), and the ninety-ninth is the highest (instead of the lowest).

A score which is often used as one of the measures in determining admission to a college is the "combined score," that is, the sum of your verbal and math SAT scores. The College Entrance Examination Board also offers achievement tests. If you have taken any of these, the results should be in your file. The achievement test scores are a record of what you have already learned in a particular academic subject as compared with others who have taken the test in this field.

The ACT is a single composite score which ranges from 1 to 35. Following is a sample list comparing ACT and SAT scores:

ACT Composite Score	SAT Combined Score
5	455
10	575
15	735
20	880
23	975
25	1050
30	1275

Data in this table are courtesy of the Bureau of Elementary and Secondary Educational Testing, New York State Department of Education.

Either the SAT or the ACT will show you where you stand compared to other potential college students. SAT scores will also show you where your greater abilities lie, in math-related subjects (mathematics, science, statistics, engineering, for example) or in language-related subjects (languages, history, English, social sciences, humanities, for example).

If you have records of a vocational preference test such as the Strong-Campbell Interest Inventory, the Kuder Preference Record, or the Edwards Personal Preference Schedule, you have an objective basis for selecting a major field of study. Such vocational preference questionnaires compare your stated preferences (such as, would you prefer to go to a concert or to a baseball game?) with those of people who have worked in various fields for a number of years. The assumption is that if you like the same kinds of things as people in a particular profession, you will probably be happy and successful in that profession. If you don't, you will probably not be happy, and you may not be successful. Obviously, these preference inventories are not perfectly accurate predictors, but they are usually much better than the average young person's impression of how well he or she will like a particular field.

Using all the information that you now have about yourself, you can go about choosing a possible career and a college.

CHOOSING A TENTATIVE CAREER

Not everyone sets his or her sights on a particular career before choosing a college, but quite a few people do, and it is a good idea to do so. The career you select should be related to your interests and abilities. Parents' wishes can't be ignored since they usually pay the tuition, but the fact that your mother wants you to become a doctor or your father is a lawyer must not be permitted to take precedence over your own aims and your personal characteristics. Even a family business which you will someday inherit should be regarded as an opportunity, not a requirement.

Above all, don't choose a career because it is the fashionable thing this year; if you do, by the time you apply to professional school, the competition for admission will be very stiff and the jobs, when you finally graduate, will be few.

In selecting a tentative career, think about the time required to finish your education. For example, a basic law degree requires seven years, a medical degree, eight. And one often needs further education in order to specialize. Such degrees, with their high cost in time and money, will be worth pursuing only if you do very well at them and will enjoy the profession very much.

Consider also the requirements for advanced education. Will you be able to get into law school, medical school, a graduate school of business administration or whatever? Look up the GPA's of recently admitted students at several professional schools in your favorite field.[3] These will give you a clue as to what you need academically if you are to be admitted. The GPA's show you what kinds of students get into professional school. If most who are admitted to advanced education in the profession you want have GPA's well above a 3.0, you will have to be a much better than average college student if you plan to pursue a career in this field. If on the other hand, they run from about 2.5 (or even lower), you can probably hope to get in even if you are only an average to good college student.

How do you decide whether you have a chance to make the grade? Your high school record as reflected in your class standing is, at this time in your life, probably the best indicator of your ability to achieve academically. It measures not only your scholastic aptitude but also your ability to discipline yourself to study. Keep in mind that the competition is stiffer in college than in high school. You know yourself best. If you are heading for a profession which requires a very high scholastic average, ask yourself: Am I willing to study very hard nearly every day for the next seven or eight years? You may decide that you are not.

---

[3] Books giving this information will probably be available in your local public library.

However, if you are ambitious but have doubts about your self-discipline and your probable college average, remember that by learning how to study, you can improve both your self-discipline and your grades.

Also don't worry if you have no particular career in mind. Many students come to college with little preference about what they will do for a living; many others change their minds before graduating. Just make sure to choose a good liberal arts college well suited to your own intellectual abilities and other needs. On the other hand, if you are a junior-college sophomore about to transfer to a four-year school, you should have a pretty clear idea of your career choices, because you do not have many semester hours left in which to meet pre-professional requirements.

SELECTING A COLLEGE

College is four years of your life, so, within the range of your financial ability, select one that is best suited to you as a person.

As everyone knows, college costs are high. So most people give close attention to what is going to come out of pocket during those four years, namely, tuition and fees, books and other supplies, living expenses at home or at school, transportation to and from school, recreation and clothing. School financial aid offices will help you to estimate expenses and will also help you to find funds to meet them. Nowadays, a substantial part of the money to pay college expenses will probably come from loans. It will be up to you to decide whether to borrow and how much to borrow. You should compare the long-run cost of college and professional school with the probable difference between your total income as a college- or professional-school graduate and your total income as only a high-school graduate. Long-run college costs should be estimated as four years of tuition and fees, books and supplies, interest on loans, plus estimated loss of pay which you would otherwise earn at a full-time job. If your chosen field requires study at the graduate level, you must add in the cost of one, two, three or four years of professional training and the loss of pay during those years, too. In making the decision whether to spend the money (including borrowing) to go to college and professional school, to four-year college, to two-year college or to some other kind of post-high school educational institution, you should consider carefully your vocational interests and your intellectual ability and self-discipline to meet the requirements.

Once you have decided how much, if any, further education you should get, choose a school suited to your own abilities and interests. Colleges vary, not only in their admissions requirements, but also in the courses of study which they offer. Furthermore, within each school, the various programs will vary in quality. Even if you have not chosen a vocation, select a college which is suited to your own capabilities. For example, if your high-school grades and a high math SAT indicate that you are likely to be good in science, choose a school which has a reputation in science studies. If you have a high verbal SAT and have always liked English, languages and social studies, look for a school which is good in the humanities and social sciences.

It is a good idea to select a college where the other students are of about the same ability as yourself. Although this is taken care of for most people by college admissions standards, top scholars sometimes get very attractive scholarship offers from schools where the average student's ability is very much below their own. If you are one of these, see if you can get financial aid from a school where the other students will be more like yourself intellectually.[4] Otherwise, you may not develop your ca-

---

[4] Some universities have an honors college in which the students have better SAT scores than the average of the university as a whole. This is a factor to be considered if you should be offered a scholarship at a school where the average student is considerably below your own ability.

Similarly, some universities have a special division which offers an opportunity to the high-school underachiever to catch up for a year before entering the larger university setting. This is a possibility for the able person who was poorly motivated or immature in high school but who has grown up and now wants to get into a college where his real abilities will be developed.

pacities to the fullest because the academic work is too easy for you, or you may do poorly because you lack the challenge needed to keep you studying.

On the other hand, athletes sometimes get attractive offers from schools where the average ability is far above their own. Even with tutorial help, they sometimes find the going very rough. Of course, if you are aiming at a career in athletics, other factors than intellectual comradeship will influence your choice.

Finally, you should consider the life style of the school. Do you find it hard to join in, make friends, get involved in campus activities? Perhaps you would be happiest at a small college where you would inevitably get to know everyone. In the same way, if you need a good deal of support from your teachers and you like to know them well, a small school may be best for you. On the other hand, if you prefer a large arena, if you want, for example, to test your political skills in the politics of a large campus, choose a big school. Some schools offer a combination of both, a small school within the framework of a considerably larger university. This might be an honors college or an innovative college which approaches liberal arts teaching differently from most schools. This kind of school may be a good choice for the student who wants the advantages of a small school but would also like to have the opportunities offered by a university, that is, a better library than most small schools can offer, a more interesting social life and a broader curriculum.

Another factor that is less considered than it once was is whether to go to a single-sex or a coeducational school. For women, especially, this is still an important consideration. Women students who tend to take the traditional feminine role may find that they are overshadowed in the classroom by men of lesser ability. Women students are also likely to run into some conscious and unconscious sex discrimination at coeducational schools. There is evidence that women who graduate from women's colleges are more successful in careers than those who graduate from coeducational schools. This is an important consideration if you are a career-oriented woman. However, if you are a relatively assertive woman and one who wants the daily company of males, choose a coed school.

These factors are probably more important than the part of the country where you study or your preferences in climate and recreation. But, if you have given thought to all these things and you still have some options concerning location, by all means satisfy your desire to be in the Far West, in a warm climate, or in ski country. After you have narrowed your choice down to two or three schools, visit each one if you can possibly afford it. Talk to the students who are already going to the school; they may be your most reliable source of information about the kind of school it is.

What if all this information about choosing a school is pointless because you are required by circumstances to go to the nearest or cheapest educational institution around? Don't stop reading now. There is more to planning than just choosing a school.

SELECTING A MAJOR

As a college freshman, you will not have to choose a major yet. However, you should begin to look around. Don't select a major just because it seems to be a good way to make a living these days. Test the water before diving in. Study the college or university bulletin. What are the requirements for the various majors you think you might undertake? Do they match with what you know about your own abilities? Have you got the high school prerequisites that you may need for some of these courses? If not, you may have to take some remedial work.

Your freshman year is a good time to try out courses in various fields to see which ones appeal to you as possible specialities. Those which you don't like very well will not be a loss. They will probably fit into the distribution requirement[5] for the major

---

[5] "Distribution requirements" are courses in the liberal arts outside your major field which you will be required to take in order to insure that you graduate with a broad-based "liberal" education.

you ultimately do select. At worst, they will count toward graduation credits as electives. If you need remedial work in English or mathematics, it is wise to take it in your freshman year. To do well in your other college studies you need what you can learn in the remedial courses.

If you are a more advanced student, you do not have the same options to test out various majors that are open to freshmen (unless you are willing to invest in an extra year in college). You must consult the requirements for the major you need to go into your chosen career. If you are a transfer, be sure to review carefully your transfer evaluation to make sure that you are getting all the credit to which you are entitled. Also, do not register without consulting fully with an advisor in your chosen major who can help you make sure that you will be able to meet all your requirements for graduation during the time in school remaining to you.

Using the suggestions made in this chapter, you—whether you are a freshman or an advanced student—should be able to choose a college suitable for your scholastic abilities. You may also have blocked out some career possibilities while considering a major field. If you have been unable to choose a career because of lack of sufficient information, or if the career you've selected has led you into courses which you don't like or do poorly in, you should take advantage of your college's career counseling service. One of the advantages of going to college is that it can help you to clarify your own educational objectives. Take advantage of what the college offers in this respect. You will have a better record in college if you get into the right field early rather than waiting until you have made a mess in one major before getting into another which suits you better.

CHAPTER III

Planning Your Semester's Work

Most schools offer education in semester, trimester or quarterly segments. As the names indicate, there are two semesters, three trimesters and four quarters in a year. Regardless of how the school year is divided, however, the student usually takes the equivalent of 30 to 32 semester-hours credit per year for a total of 120 to 128 semester hours at graduation. A semester hour equals one class hour per week for fourteen or fifteen weeks. (The last week may be set aside for final exams.) Most courses will be either 3 semester hours or 4 semester hours, depending on how the school course load is divided. Assuming that your school is on the semester plan (the most common), you will be taking 15 or 16 semester hours each semester if you are making normal progress toward graduation. You should plan each semester so as to make some progress on specific graduation requirements while keeping your study load to a size you can handle comfortably. This means that you must balance the courses which will be hard for you and will require a lot of study time with courses which will be reasonably easy.

PLANNING SEMESTER
COURSE LOAD

To plan your semester course load well requires a knowledge of both courses and teachers. (You already have, of course, a file of information on yourself.) If you are an entering student, you may find this hard to acquire. College bulletins offer brief descriptions of the courses given in that year, but these are relatively useless to a student trying to figure out how much work a course requires. No professor is going to say of a course: "This is a pipe I teach. Any fool can get at least a B in it." Nor is he or she going to say: "This is my shakedown course; I make a point of failing at least 20 percent of every class." A source of information better than the college bulletin may be the teachers who are orally quite candid about the difficulty of their courses. Unfortunately, they are often not around when you must decide whether to take one of their courses of some other.

Many schools publish course and teacher evaluations. When these are done entirely (including cost of publication) by students, the evaluations may be quite frank about the kind and amount of work the teacher expects, as well as whether he or she is fairly interesting or a deadly bore. Teacher evaluations published by the school itself may be less candid, but they should be consulted. A careful analysis of the previous students' answers to the questions on the evaluations of the courses you are considering can give you quite a bit of useful information concerning a particular course and teacher.

Other student's verbal opinions are another source of information on courses and teachers. However, for the person just coming in, even this source will be inadequate; to evaluate what another student says about a teacher, you really ought to know something about the aims, abilities and seriousness of the student.

Always ask the person who has been assigned to you as advisor about the courses you plan to take. Often he or she knows or can find out if a course has a heavy reading load and what it will require in terms of abilities and previous education. Do not be afraid to discuss your academic strengths and weaknesses with your advisor. The school is anxious to keep you; your tuition is now part of its budget. So rely on your advisor to help you make wise course decisions. Every reasonable accommodation will be made to help you do well and graduate creditably.

Entering students, whether freshmen or transfers, are wise to take a *minimum* full load (15 to 16 semester hours per semester). Using everything you know about yourself and all the information you can get on proposed courses and teachers, balance what promise to be difficult courses with a good sprinkling of easy ones until you have a fairly good understanding of how much work this college is going to require of you. If the semester proves easy, next time load up on the tough stuff and stretch your mind. Otherwise, continue to balance your courses.

One rule is good whether you are a freshman or an experienced college student. Start the registration process early. Schools nowadays try as much as is feasible to equalize the course enrollments so as to cut costs by keeping all the full-time faculty busy. Therefore, they usually place an upper limit on the number of students in each course in order to force students from the more popular into the less popular courses. (Limits on the number of students in each course may also be made necessary by the limitations on numbers of classrooms and of individual classroom seating.) If you want to be sure to get the courses you have picked out, register as early as possible. Let someone else be the late-comer who is forced to take an unpopular course.

PLANNING YOUR STUDY
LOAD TO KEEP UP YOUR GPA

Planning what courses to take in a semester is only a beginning. You must continue to plan your study load so as to establish and maintain a good grade-point average (GPA). Grade-point average is computed by multiplying the number of semester hours in a course by a figure representing the value of the grade you get, adding up the resulting numbers and dividing them by the total number of semester hours. For exampke, if A = 4, B = 3, C = 2, D = 1, F = 0:

Course	Semester Hours	Grade	Quality Points
Eng. Lit.	3	B	9
French II	3	C	6
Poli. Sci. I	3	A	12
Anthro. II	3	F	0
Biology I	3	D	3
Totals	15		30
			Grade Point Average = 2.0

If you are to maintain a good GPA,[1] you must make certain at the outset that, for all your care in selecting courses, you have not gotten in over your head academically. Two options are available to you if you have, the Drop/Add option and the Pass/Fail option.

If you are doubtful about your ability to handle any of your courses, try to make sure at the very beginning of the semester that you will be able to manage what you have undertaken. *Buy your texts immediately* (at the college book store), *but do not put your name or any other mark in them.* Instead, browse through them and, consulting your course syllabi,[2] estimate how much time you will require to complete the typical weekly assignment. Be sure to consider, also, the papers and outside readings. If the work load in any course seems to be *substantially* more than you can handle, or if any textbook seems so far over your head

---

[1] The definition of "good GPA" depends on what you are planning to do. If all you want is to graduate from college, a 2.0 will barely suffice. If you are planning to go to law or medical school, a GPA of better than 3.0 is desirable. Check admissions requirements for the professional or graduate schools in your chosen profession for an idea of the desirable GPA.

[2] A course *syllabus* is an outline of the course giving required reading and writing assignments, the schedule of examinations and sometimes other information, too. Syllabi are usually handed out at the first meetings of courses.

that you will not be able to understand it even after considerable effort, *drop* that course immediately and *add* something easier. It is much wiser to do this at the beginning of the semester than to wait until later and end up with a low grade, an incomplete or a withdrawal on your record. Most schools permit changes in registration at the beginning of a semester without recording it on a student's transcript. Furthermore, if you make this decision early and you have not written in your textbook, the college book store will exchange it for another book or for a refund. Finally, making a change promptly insures that you will miss as little as possible of the course you substitute for the one which was too hard.

Just one word of caution—don't drop out too easily. College courses are designed to stretch your mind; so drop a course only if it seems to you that you really won't be able to manage it. Consider also whether the course you are dropping is a requirement. If so and you drop it, you will have to take it at some later time. Perhaps it would be wiser to try it now and, if necessary, drop it later in the semester. Many schools make it possible to drop a course without penalty up until the middle of the semester, and, in some places, one can drop a course without penalty at any time before the final exam. But "without penalty" means you will not get an F if you drop; it does not mean that there will be no mark on your transcript to show that you withdrew. Professional-school admissions officers keep their eyes open for numerous withdrawals, so try to do your withdrawing early enough to prevent it showing on your record. Besides, you get no tuition rebate for a course dropped in mid-semester.

If you get into a course you can pass but in which you think you are not going to get a good grade, try the Pass/Fail option. Pass grades are not taken into account in computing the GPA. Note, however, that a failing grade in a P/F course will count against you. A change from a letter grade (usually, A, B, C, D or F) to a P/F option is usually permitted until a few weeks into the semester so if a course proves more difficult than you expected, you can opt for P/F. It is, of course, also possible to opt for Pass/Fail when registering for a course, provided the course is included within the Pass/Fail option. Most schools limit the number of P/F grades and often exclude them entirely in one's major field.[3]

Wisely exercised, the Drop/Add and the Pass/Fail options can protect you against F, D or even C grades. But don't overdo them; professional and graduate schools take them into account when deciding whether or not to admit a student, especially one who is otherwise on the borderline.

Once you have settled finally on your program for the semester, begin planning how you are going to get all the work done. The rule of thumb which professors are supposed to follow in making assignments is two hours outside work for each hour of class. The number of class hours normally equals the number of semester hours assigned to the course. The exceptions to this are laboratory courses which often have more class hours per week, including lab time, than is assigned in semester-hours credit. A 3 semester-hour course would, in theory, require nine hours of work per week, three in class and six outside. However, different professors often have very different ideas of what six hours work is. And one student can read in an hour what may very well take another three hours.

Note which courses require long papers and when they are due. Plan to start on them as soon as possible. It is wise to speak to your teachers about any requirements respecting papers during the first or second week of the term. Also, ask your teachers or find out from other students which teachers will grade you down for papers that are handed in late and which ones will not. Start on the tough teachers' papers first, of course, but don't put off the others too long. Remember, sooner or later, all the papers will have to be written. An incomplete at the end of this semester—unless you will make it up during the intersession—will only make the next semester more difficult. Also, incompletes, if not made up, become F's.

During the first week of the semester, make an estimate of

---

[3] A few courses will probably be mandatory Pass/Fail; i.e., the letter-grade option will not be available.

the total work you will have to accomplish during the semester. This involves adding up all the pages in your assigned textbooks and other readings. In making this estimate, distinguish among "skills-course" readings which require intensive study (such as elementary English, math or language texts and lab manuals), "content-course" readings which are largely informational and require less intense concentration, and outside readings which are usually the least time-consuming.[4] Division by the number of weeks in the semester will give you an idea of your average weekly load for each kind of reading. Then note the number and length of the papers to be done. Following is an illustration of such an estimate:

Course Name	Content Readings	Skills Readings	Outside Readings	Papers[a]
Eng. Lit.	754		about 800	9–15 pp.
Poli. Sci.	595		about 375	10–15 pp.
Anthropology	484		about 15	5–10 pp.
Biology	355	155		
French		250 (grammar)		
		325 (readings)		
Totals	2188	730	1190	24–40 pp.
Weeks	14	14	14	
Per week	156	52	85	

[a] 3 English essays, 3–5 pp. each; 1 Poli. Sci. research paper, 10–15 pp.; 1 Anthropology research paper, 5–10 pp.

When completed, this summary may be a bit of a shock. It should be. The idea is to shock yourself into getting started promptly. You cannot expect your college teachers to prod you as your high school teachers may have done. No one is going to remind you if you don't go to class, fail to do your reading and never hand in a paper; you may think that you have been forgotten completely until you receive a transcript full of F grades.

---

[4] See Chapter V, "Reading for College Courses," for a discussion of the various kinds of reading.

So it is up to you to keep after yourself to do your reading, to go to class and to write your papers. Paste the estimate of your total semester's work in the front of your notebook where it can serve as a constant reminder of work to be done. If you check off tasks as they are accomplished, it will also serve as a record of progress.

KEEPING YOURSELF WORKING

Unfortunately, with time, you may get so used to the estimate in the front of your notebook that you won't even see it. So you must force yourself to be conscious of what remains to be done. The best way to do this is to make a weekly list of tasks to be accomplished.

The weekly list—which must, of course, be prepared every week—reminds you of the actual work to be accomplished in the near future. It also serves as a motivation to do the work. Below is an example of such a list:

Week of October 10–16
English Lit.
  Finish reading *King Lear*.
  Begin essay on "The Lilliputians."
French
  Review adjective agreement (Quiz?).
  Study the tenses of *avoir* and *être* (especially the past subjunctive).
  Learn next 50 vocabulary words.
  Finish to p. 75 in *Readings*. . . .
Poli. Sci.
  Read section on political parties.
  Continue research for "Tweed and Tammany Hall."
  Finish Neustadt, *Presidential Power*.

Anthropology
> Read chapter on "Early Man in Africa," pp. 144–190.
> Find topic for paper. Note: Ask prof if I can do something on the Dawson fraud.

Biology
> Finish experiment with fruit flies.
> Finish chapter on genetic inheritance.

As you work your way through a list like the one above, checking off the tasks will give you a small feeling of satisfaction which will reinforce you to keep working. In estimating your weekly load, you may find it helpful to overestimate a little bit how much you can accomplish; a slight feeling of anxiety is a helpful prod to getting work done. Furthermore, should you be successful in getting more done than you really need to, you will be a little ahead, so that, when you do take a day off to go skiing or something of the kind, you won't fall impossibly far behind.

If you find yourself having trouble finishing your weekly list, supplement it with a daily list of tasks. Each day's list can be broken down into hours, so that you can plan exactly when you are going to study what. As you will see in the next chapter, different kinds of tasks should be fitted into different size time slots. Furthermore, daily planning makes it possible to take with you each morning exactly those books and materials which you will need to best utilize your time during the school day.

THE ADVANTAGES OF PLANNING

Regular planning offers a number of advantages over simply taking things as they come. It helps you to choose your courses realistically in terms of your own needs and abilities. It allows you to foresee problems so as to take advantage of registration and grading options to protect your GPA. It also helps you to keep track of where you are in your semester's work. Finally, it acts as a spur to keep working. Planning is essential to success; get in the habit of it.

CHAPTER IV

Using Study Time Effectively

Those who do not study well usually display one or more of the following faults in the use of study time: not allowing enough time; not using the time available appropriately; not concentrating effectively during the time used.

ALLOWING ENOUGH TIME FOR STUDY

Probably the commonest fault in the use of study time is not allowing enough of it for the tasks which must be accomplished. This may be a matter of personal need or simply of self-indulgence. In either case, one does not value one's education highly enough. Other, more highly valued activities take away from study time.

One of these is working for pay. It is hard to argue with those who need to work to eat. But, if you are spending so much time earning a living that you cannot finish your school work, you need to rearrange your life. Talk to the financial aid advisors at your school; often they can help you to get a scholarship, a low-cost loan or some other form of financial help which will enable you to cut back on your work schedule and devote more time to study.

On the other hand, if you are working more than you can

afford just to drive a sportier car or to support a more expensive wardrobe, you are selling out your future for a jazzier present. Examine your priorities; maybe you should quit school for a while and just work. When you have saved enough money or are ready to cut back your standard of living in exchange for an education, return to school.

Maybe you are wasting your time because you have very little motivation to study. You value partying, gossiping or campus politics more than you do education. It could be that you have not chosen courses which correspond to your own abilities and interests. Talk to your advisor about making changes before it is too late. If you are majoring in business administration when your real interest is music, change your major. If the problem is that you are simply bored with school, perhaps you should quit before wasting any more of your parents' or your own money.

Finally, you may simply not realize how much time is needed, or you may be wasting time without realizing how it can be used. In that case, you need to learn how to use your time better.

USING AVAILABLE TIME
APPROPRIATELY

Study time comes in segments—maybe an hour between classes (actually good for about fifty minutes), possibly ten minutes while waiting in the dentist's office, a three-hour segment between the end of your 1:00 P.M. class and the beginning of your 5:00 P.M. class, two or three hours Saturday morning before you go to work, and so on.

To study effectively, you must fit the task to the segment of time available. If you should try to read a long Supreme Court decision in ten-minute time segments, you would lose track of the argument in the intervals from one time segment to the next. On the other hand, you would get bored to death reading over and over to yourself for four hours 50 new vocabulary words to be memorized. These are extreme cases, of course, but they illustrate the point that it is necessary to make a preliminary judgment as to how long a task will take you and to undertake to do it when you have sufficient time, neither less nor more than is needed.

Except just before exams, very long time segments—four hours or more—are best used for accomplishing the research for papers. Research requires time to pursue a subject; to search first for sources of information; to look for the needed books or articles in the library; to skim through the books or articles for the desired information; then to take notes on the information itself. If you don't set aside enough time, you may have to stop work to go to class when the chase is hottest, that is, when you have almost got what you want. So save your Saturday afternoons, your Sundays or your dateless evenings for this job.

Medium-length periods—50 minutes, an hour and a half, two hours—are well adapted to reading and study in your textbooks. Try to judge the time you will need to read each chapter or section and plan to cover that part when you have available a time segment of the right length. If you keep a daily list of tasks to be accomplished, write opposite each task the time when you expect to get it done. If you don't do this in writing, do it mentally.

Try to plan your reading so that you finish what you have set out to do in the time you have allowed yourself. Breaking off in the middle of a task is frustrating, and frustration is not rewarding. You should finish a task; then you will feel good about the doing of it. If you need to press yourself a little bit to finish, do so. Ultimately, that will improve your reading speed.

However, it is important to note that when a task needs intense concentration to achieve understanding, a time segment of from an hour and a half to three hours will be needed, even if the number of pages to be read is not very great. The reason for this is that about a half hour of study is required to work up to a state of intense concentration. Once there, you should not stop studying for at least an hour.

Conversely, be prepared to take advantage of short segments of time by carrying with you at all times a set of 3×5 cards.

These should be used for any kind of work which can be subdivided into very small parts and recorded in a small space. Some rote learning is of this kind. For example, studying the vocabulary of a foreign language, of ordinary English, or of a new discipline[1] is best done in short periods of time. Write each word that you need to learn on one side of a card. On the other side, write the definition. The same can be done with mathematical, statistical or chemical formulas or any other information which needs to be memorized and can be easily recorded on 3 x 5 cards. Memorization of short bits of information is very dull work and is best done in small time segments, that is, five minutes to a half hour. Most likely to be wasted is time that comes in less than half-hour segments, so acquiring the habit of using these short periods of time will save you a lot in longer periods.

Again planning is the key. Get into the habit of planning your work ahead for each day. Carry with you those materials and books which will make it possible for you to best use the time segments that come your way during the day.

CONCENTRATING ON THE
TASK AT HAND

One problem which faces a great many students who set a high value on education and provide themselves with the time for study is that they cannot concentrate when they sit down to do their work. If you have trouble concentrating, here are a few suggestions that may help you.

Keep your body and brain in good shape. Most of us are familiar with the phenomenon that concentration is difficult when we are ill or in pain. (On the other hand, intense concentration can make one unconscious of pain.) Fever interferes with concentration; so does fatigue. So it is necessary to stay in good health and to get adequate exercise and sleep. Although an intense need

---

[1] In scholars' language, a discipline is a field of study.

to learn will often override the need for sleep, it is probably unwise to undertake difficult study tasks when you are tired or ill. If you have been quite ill and need extra rest to get well again, it may be a good idea to cut back on your studies by dropping a course or two until you are back on your feet. This is expensive in money but may save you from lowering your GPA.

Drugs also prevent concentration. Alcohol and marijuana do not mix well with study. The same is certainly true of the harder drugs—angel dust, heroin, and so on. Tobacco, also, is probably bad for concentration since it constricts the blood vessels and cuts down on oxygen to the brain. The addicted smoker will not agree, however, as his need to smoke interferes with his will to concentrate. This book is not intended as a sermon against tobacco and drugs. However, use common sense about such self-indulgence. A sensible balance between study and recreation is needed if study is to be most effective. You must make the decision about the balance and whether drugs will be a part of your recreation—which drugs and how much of them.

Assuming that your brain is clear, find a quiet place. Noise is distracting and interferes with concentration. If you live in a dormitory and your roommate is noisy or likes to play the radio or TV or just to chat, go to the library. Most college libraries stay open until 10:00 P.M. or later, and quiet is enforced by the librarians.

Eliminate other distractions. If you are at home or in your dorm room, put your fascinating novel out of sight; turn off the TV and the radio; ask your friends not to call you at your regular study time. Put aside worries about other tasks. Your study plan should reassure you that your work will get done if you follow the plan. Put other worries out of your mind, too. Letting them interfere with your studies cannot help you.

Now your mind is clear and you are ready to concentrate. To concentrate means to give all your attention to a subject, to get completely involved in it. Ability to concentrate intensely, especially on difficult materials, may be partly a matter of "native intelligence," but it is certainly also partly a matter of skill and can be learned with practice. Most of all, concentration seems to be related to your degree of interest. Finally, concentration is partly a matter of *intention* to give complete attention to what you are studying.

So intend to concentrate. Overcome your reluctance to sit down with the book or paper by doing it. Then give your mind to the task and *try* to get interested. If you are not interested, analyze why. Lack of interest can be caused by difficulty in understanding the material. Make a point of understanding it. Look up the words which bother you (and write them on 3 x 5 cards for future memorization). Read the difficult passages aloud to yourself slowly, several times if necessary. If a paragraph eludes you, reread the paragraph preceding it and the paragraph following it; then reread it. Read it again. If necessary go back and reread the entire section. Each time you read the material it will become a little bit clearer to you, but you must make an effort to understand; otherwise, you will just be reading words. Take notes.[2] Formulate a question or two to raise in class concerning the difficult section and write the questions down. It is important to use as many senses as possible in attempting to understand. The brain seems to work better when we use several different ways of presenting it with an idea to be understood and remembered. Reading aloud to yourself uses both vision and hearing. Taking notes forces you to think and uses the kinetic[3] sense. Formulating a question to ask in class forces your brain to get at the essential ideas, and writing the questions down reinforces these ideas by using the kinetic sense again. By this time, you may understand the difficult passage well enough that you won't need to ask the question you made up.

But what if the material is just plain boring? This is a more persistent problem than is difficult material. You find yourself reading just words in order to complete your self-assigned task

---

[2] See Chapter V for methods.
[3] *Kinetic* as used here means resulting from motion.

but not really understanding or caring that you do not. You count pages still to be read, sigh, groan and suffer acute boredom, wishing only that you were done. Maybe you need a break. If so, take one. Another remedy is to take notes but to take them sparingly, not copiously. Ask yourself what is worth remembering. Is this idea important? Does it add enough to some larger concept to be worth remembering. Try to get the major ideas of the chapter or section down in the fewest possible words. This will force you to think about what you are doing.

As you learn more about a subject, your interest will almost certainly increase. The subject matter will become more meaning-ful, and relationships to other subjects not mentioned in the text will occur to you. But first you must make the effort to get inter-ested.

The skill of concentration requires practice. If you have been away from academic study for a considerable time, or if you have never had to concentrate very hard, you may find it hard to concentrate for long periods, even on material which interests you. The practiced person may take a few minutes up to a half hour to get to a peak level of concentration, but he or she can usually continue to concentrate for several hours at a stretch. The person who is learning how will not concentrate so easily, nor reach such a high peak nor be able to maintain concentration for such a long period of time. He or she will probably have to take breaks at approximately hourly intervals. You can tell when you need a break because you will become conscious of your body, hunger, a cramped foot, tired eyes, and so forth. Stop and rest. Walk outside and get some fresh air. But keep your rests brief; otherwise, you will not be able to get back quickly to your peak of concentration when you return to work.

As you learn to concentrate, you will find your willingness to study increasing. Your periods of concentration will tend to be longer. To lengthen these periods even further, try to increase the time between breaks by forcing yourself to an extra five min-utes work. Slowly you can train yourself to be a better concentrator, and, as you do, you will become a more interested, more highly motivated student. Inevitably, your grades will improve.

USING YOUR NON-CONSCIOUS MIND

Once you have learned to concentrate, you can begin to deliberately use your non-conscious[4] mind to work for you. When you are working on a problem which is very difficult to understand or the solution eludes you, concentrate on it hard; think about different possible solutions; go over the problem a number of times looking for clues to the answer. If it doesn't come, go for a walk, go to sleep, take a break; but don't get involved in another task or engrossing amusement. Let your mind rest. Your brain will continue to work on the problem though you will not be conscious of it. Then suddenly an idea will come, and often it will be the right answer. Eureka! This technique, once you master it, will be especially valuable to you when you are involved in a creative task, writing a paper for example.

USING CONCENTRATION

The art of concentration is probably the most valuable skill you can acquire. The ability to concentrate overlaps all the other skills you may have and can be applied to any area requiring thought, including the physical arts. It is an absolute necessity to anyone who plans to engage in a thinking profession—science, law, medicine, engineering. If you plan to go into any field requiring deep concentration, you must work constantly on *learning*

---

[4] I use the term *non-conscious* to distinguish the phenomenon I am about to describe from the Freudian term *unconscious* or the older psychological term *sub-conscious*.

to concentrate. Your determination to succeed will be important in this task. Only you can give yourself that.

MAKING THE USE OF STUDY
TIME REWARDING

The emphasis throughout this chapter has been to plan for sufficient time and to use it effectively. Using time effectively is rewarding in several ways. First, it will result in better grades. Second, it will make more time available for other things that you want to do. Third, it will result in a feeling of accomplishment. Ultimately, the feeling of accomplishment will make study itself more pleasant, and this, in turn, will make effective use of time easier.

CHAPTER V

Reading for College Courses

Reading is undoubtedly the most important skill for doing well in college. But not all reading is alike. It ranges from the lightest kind of amusement to extremely deep concentration. In reading for a course in school, understanding and remembering are essential, and the ways of reading for school vary depending upon what one is reading and one's purpose in reading it. In the following chapter we will deal with the structure of a textbook and then discuss the problem of remembering what the book said for the three most common types of college course readings: content-course texts, skills-course texts and outside readings.

STRUCTURE OF A TEXTBOOK

The structure of a textbook is planned to enhance understanding of its content. It is divided and subdivided into sections and subsections, each with a title or a heading, so that it is easy to see the organization and the relationship among the ideas.

Book Titles

The title and subtitle of a textbook tell you what is the major subject-matter of the book and what its main emphasis is. For instance, the title of this book, *Getting Good Grades*, tells you that the subject is making a good academic record, and the subtitle, *How to Succeed in College,* says that the book will tell you how to do it.

Table of Contents

Listed in the Table of Contents of a textbook are section titles (if any), chapter titles and sometimes chapter subtitles, with a page reference for each chapter. These titles tell you what are the major subdivisions of the book. Some tables of contents also list the major subdivisions of the chapters. A study of the Table of Contents will not only tell you where to find the beginning of each chapter, it will also give you a pretty good overview of the material in the textbook.

Chapters and Their Subdivisions

Each chapter of a book is concerned with one major idea which is indicated by its title. Chapters are, in turn, subdivided into sections, each identified by a heading. Longer sections will probably be divided into subsections and so on. Subsections and sub-subsections often have their own subheadings or sub-subheadings. A title, heading or subheading is a phrase which conveys the major idea that is discussed in that part of the chapter. The importance of a section, subsection or sub-subsection within a chapter can be determined by the position and typeface of its heading. For example, in this book, chapter titles are printed in large boldface, italic letters and are centered just below the chapter number. Chapter section headings are centered, all in capital letters and are in boldface (very black) type. Subsection headings are centered, have the first letter of each major word capitalized and are in boldface type. Sub-subsection headings are indented and on the same line that begins the paragraph. If you were to copy these titles and headings, subordinating them according to their location on the page and their typeface, you would have a fairly complete outline of this book. When reading a textbook, it is helpful to become familiar with the location and typeface of the various section and subsection headings because they show the logical relationship among the ideas. Consequently, they are a very useful guide both in the initial reading and in later review.

Text

The textual part of the book—that part which is written in sentences and paragraphs—expands the ideas in the headings. The first paragraph of a subdivision introduces the general topic which that subdivision deals with; later paragraphs expand the idea.

To understand a paragraph, you should be able to pick out its topic sentence easily. Frequently, the topic sentence comes at the beginning. For example, the very first sentence on page 1 of this book gives the topic of that first paragraph (and of the whole book). However, a book would be very dull reading if the topic sentence were to be found at the beginning of every paragraph. So the topic sentence may be found anywhere in a paragraph. For example, in the second paragraph of the topic "A Skill to be Learned" on page 2 of this book, the first sentence is a lead-in sentence, and the second sentence gives the topic:

> "We know also that regular study is an important part of getting good grades. *Because regular study is a habit, it too can be learned.*"

A topic sentence may even be at the end of a paragraph. The first paragraph of Chapter III (p. 14) presents its topic in the culminating sentence:

> *"This means that you must balance the courses which will be hard for you and will require a lot of study time with courses which will be reasonably easy."*

Because the topic sentence may be found anywhere in a paragraph, you cannot get all the ideas in a book by reading only the first sentence of each paragraph. However, with a bit of practice, you can learn to pick out the topic sentences quickly and easily.

To some readers, this explanation of the structure of a textbook may seem unduly elementary. However, consciousness of textbook structure will help you to develop three important skills: an ability to determine quickly the major content of a book; an ability to skim a chapter or section to find the specific idea you are interested in; and an ability to organize your own expository writing logically and coherently.

Tables and Illustrations

Tables and graphs, pictures and other illustrations are included in a textbook as aids to understanding and, sometimes, with a view to making it more entertaining. Get in the habit of studying these and understanding what they are saying. Most students are glad to look at pictures or cartoons, but they tend to pass over the tables and graphs. Generally, this is because they have not learned to read them easily. Following are brief discussions of the reading of tables and graphs.

Tables. Tables condense information so that a great deal of it can be included in a small space. They are arranged so that it is easy to compare the figures within them. Figures are arranged in columns and rows. Columns are labeled at the top and at the rows on the left side. On page 36 is a simple table which illustrates the major parts to be found in any table. It is extremely important to get in the habit of reading the tables in a textbook. Not only do they give information which the author of the text thinks important, but the ability to read tables is a skill every literate person should have.

Graphs. A graph is a picture of some kind of relationship which can be expressed in two (or sometimes more) dimensions. For example, the graph on page 37 depicts the growth over time of the student body at Guildenstern University. Graphs are of many kinds, and it is beyond the scope of this book to describe them in detail. Different disciplines develop different kinds of

TABLE I

Students Attending Guildenstern University, By College or Division—1977–78		Title

University Subdivision	Number	Percent of Total	Column Head
Liberal Arts			Stub
Social Sciences	945	29.3	
Humanities	432	13.4	
Natural Sciences	105	3.3	
School of Business	782	24.2	
School of Education	543	16.8	
School of Law	253	7.8	
Medical School	125	3.9	
At large	45	1.4	
Total	3,230	100.1[a]	

Source: Data in this table are imaginary.
[a] Percentages do not total 100 owing to rounding.

graphs to illustrate the relationships they are trying to explain. It is important to study and understand every graph in a textbook. If you find that you cannot understand a graph or any other illustration in a textbook, ask your teacher to explain it. Failure to understand a graph indicates a failure to understand either the relationship it conveys or the method involved in creating it. Literate people are able to read graphs.

Notes

Like other academic volumes, textbooks have notes, although they usually have fewer than most other scholarly works. A note is signaled in one of two ways: when a number follows a word or a sentence and is located a half line above it, thus[1]; when a parenthesis follows a word or sentence and introduces a name of an author, title or, occasionally, a page number which is then followed by a closing parenthesis, thus (Aghassi, p. 20). Notes have two purposes, either to make references or to expand the

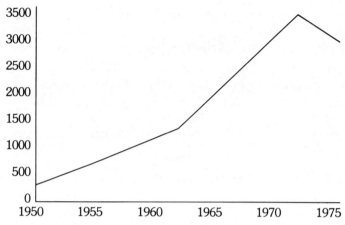

CHART I: Growth of Guildenstern University, 1950–1975.
(Data are imaginary.)

content. Reference notes either cite the authority for statements made in the text or make cross references within it. Content notes make comments upon or expand the material given in a passage. A note which is at the bottom of a page is called a footnote. Other places where notes may be found in textbooks are at the end of each chapter or, arranged by chapters, at the end of the book. These are known as endnotes.

Get accustomed to the noting pattern in the books you read. Even though their information is not important enough to include in the "text" of your textbook, much valuable information is contained in notes. Some of the most interesting material in a textbook is found in the content notes, and reference notes are an excellent source of information about books and articles where further data about the subject which is noted can be found. Get into the habit of reading notes.

Appendixes

When an author has some material that is important but does not fit well in the text of a textbook, he or she will often put in into an appendix. This book, for example, has two appendixes, one on the tools which a student needs and one on how to use the library. Appendixes often have essential information. Statistics texts, for example, often have appendixes which must be used in doing many of the problems. Find out what is in the appendixes, if any, of your textbooks; they may contain necessary material. They always contain material which the author thought important enough to include.

Index

One of the most useful parts of any book of information is the index which tells you where to find specific data. Indexes organize the facts and ideas in a book in alphabetical order and give the pages where particular facts or ideas may be found. Some books have more than one index, an index of authors, for example, and a subject index. Law books usually have two indexes, one for subjects and one for cases cited. This book has only one index. You should use an index whenever you want to find out quickly what a book has to say about a particular person, event, idea or fact.

Some textbooks do not include all the parts described above. Often a text contains no information that is suitable for an appendix. A few texts—fortunately not many—have no index. In some fields, tables and graphs are not needed to supplement the textual information. However, every student should be familiar with each of these information aids as well as with the general structure of a textbook. Not to be able to use them all is to be less than a good reader.

REMEMBERING WHAT THE
BOOK SAYS

It is very important to remember what the books you read have to say. But what you need to remember and how you go about remembering varies considerably with the nature of the course and the function the book plays in the course.

Content-Course Textbooks

Content courses are those which give the student a large amount of information about the ideas and facts that are indispensable to an understanding of the part of a discipline designated by the title of the course. For example, a course entitled "History of American Political Parties" would deal with many of the facts concerning political parties, both major and minor, in the American past. A textbook for such a course would undoubtedly contain information about a great many of these facts and also about some concepts developed to explain the particular history and characteristics of American political parties. Such a textbook would probably be quite fat. Content-course textbooks do tend to be fat, often running upwards of four or five hundred pages.

How does one remember so much? Obviously one does not remember every word; the objective is to remember the main ideas and the facts to support them. Students properly think of this problem in terms of various methods of putting these facts and ideas in such a form that they are easily remembered. There are two ways to do this; either underline the most important ideas in the book or take notes.

If you own the textbook and have ample time for review, it may be feasible simply to underline the most important parts of it. Undoubtedly, this is a faster way to get the reading done than note taking. Its popularity is made clear by the large variety of colored pens available for just this purpose. You can go over the material first with red, then underline parts of the red with yellow, reinforce the yellow with green and so on. If you are going to use this technique for remembering, make a point of underlining only the topic sentences and such explanatory material as you *must* have to understand the topic. Making an effort to limit yourself in this way keeps your mind on the subject and helps to avoid stressing too much material. Unfortunately, as a method designed to help you remember, underlining has two weaknesses: First, you are likely to underline too much and thus have too much to review before examinations; second, the process of underlining does very little in itself to help you remember.

A better method, if time does not press too much during the semester, is to take notes. The most effective way to absorb the main ideas and facts in a textbook is to outline it. Use a formal outline structure as follows:

I. Chapter I—Title
  A.
    1.
      a.
      b.
    2.
    3.
      a.
      b.
      c.
      d.
        1)
        2)
          a)
          b)
  B.
II. Chapter II—Title

The structure of the textbook in chapters, sections, subsections and sub-subsections of chapters will give you the major points and subpoints. More detailed parts of the outline will come from the topic sentences of the paragraphs. Be sure to include any definitions or illustrations which are necessary to understanding.

The disadvantage of note taking is that it is more time-consuming than underlining. The advantages are that: (1) The very process of taking notes helps you to anchor the material in your mind; (2) outlining a text helps you to see the relationships among ideas; and (3) the notes are shorter and easier to review than the book itself.

It is possible to work out a compromise between the two, outlining only those parts of a text which are the most difficult to understand and require the most concentration.

Skills-Course Textbooks

A skills course is one in which the skills and information learned serve as tools to do work in other courses. For example, English grammar and spelling are tools for writing papers in history. Statistics is a tool for investigating causes and effects in social science and the natural sciences. The most common skills courses[1] at the college level are English, mathematics, statistics, elementary foreign languages and science laboratory courses. Skills-course textbooks consist of statements of principles, examples and problems, and usually relatively little factual matter. Examples are grammar books, mathematics and statistics texts, and laboratory manuals. Skills-course textbooks are usually thin, about 150 to 200 pages. Your teacher will assign a few pages in the text to be studied and problems or exercises to be done as homework and handed in at class.

Assignments in skills-course texts are usually much shorter in number of pages than those in content texts. This is because skills texts require much more concentrated study than content texts. To study such a text, read the principle and the explanation carefully, making sure that you understand. Then do the assigned problems. Some texts give answers to some of the problems. For example, a statistics text might have an appendix giving the answers to all the even-numbered problems. Under that circumstance, your teacher would probably assign only odd-numbered problems for homework.[2] If you find a particular concept is difficult to master, don't do only the assigned homework, do some additional problems from those for which the answers are given. Then check yourself. In developing a new skill, there is no substitute for practice.

---

[1] Skills courses become content courses at more advanced levels.

[2] Your teacher will have the answers to the odd-numbered problems in a separate "Teacher's Manual" issued by the publisher.

In learning a discipline which involves a new skill, it is essential to master each section before going on to the next because understanding of each new concept usually depends on thorough mastery of what has gone before. Depending on the discipline, it may be necessary to memorize not only the concepts themselves, but also definitions and/or formulas. Therefore, the method of taking notes appropriate for a content textbook will not do for a skills textbook. Much of the material covered will not require note taking at all because it will be quite short. However, if there are any concepts, definitions or formulas which you have not thoroughly mastered, write them on 3 x 5 cards. Do not put more than one concept, one definition or one formula on a card. If a right answer exists, it should be put on the back of the card. For example, if you are striving for mastery of vocabulary, write the vocabulary word on one side of the card and the definition on the other. It is wise to keep vocabulary cards in alphabetical order.

The following illustrations show the two sides of a vocabulary card for an elementary French course:

```
French



                                    la maison



```

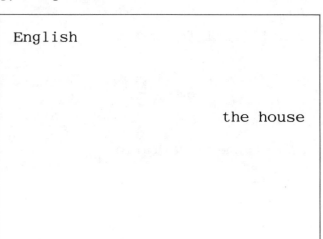

```
English



                              the house
```

Following are illustrated two sides of a formula card for an elementary statistics course:

```
Statistical concept



            standard deviation
            of a sample
```

Statistical formula

$$SD = \sqrt{\frac{\Sigma X^2}{N}}$$

SD = standard deviation
Σ = sum of
x = deviation from the mean
N = sample size

Use rubber bands to separate the cards for different courses and keep the cards in a paper cardholder. Carry them in your pocket or briefcase and use your short periods of study time (5 minutes to a half hour) for reviewing them.

Outside Readings

Outside readings are those which are required in addition to your text. Often your teachers will put on reserve in the library reserve room books or articles which are to be read for their major ideas. Or they may simply give you a reading list from which you are to select a specified number of items to be read "outside."

Outside readings do not require as careful study as either of the two kinds of textbooks. Frequently, they are books or articles by "authorities" in the discipline, that is, by people who have made important contributions to knowledge in the field. Some of these books may be classics.

Classics. If the author of your outside reading has been dead for some time, his or her book or article would not have been assigned unless it had become a classic. In that case, it is probably important because the ideas in it have been of historical importance to the development of knowledge in that field. The ideas in it may or may not still be accepted by the authorities in that discipline. For example, Lucretius, *De Rerum Natura* (On the Nature of Things) presents atomic theory which is of interest because the author was an ancient Roman whose work was a forerunner of our modern atomic theory; but his theory is thoroughly out of date and not to be accepted as is.

Classics always have a fairly long introduction by the editor. *Read it with great care and take notes on it.* It will usually summarize the author's ideas and, also, give you the editor's view of the place of the author in the history of the discipline. Classics are sometimes very difficult to read because the manner of thinking may have changed greatly from the author's day to our own. If the classic is in English of some centuries ago (and hence has not been translated), you may find the going quite tough because the meanings of some of the words will have changed as, indeed, will have some of the punctuation, syntax, spelling and capitalization. Struggle with it. The very things that make it difficult will give you new insights into ways of thinking about the world and will make you more critical of modern thought. Besides, one mark of an educated person is a familiarity with the classics.

One question is sure to come up with respect to a classic. Is it O.K. to use the published notes on a book rather than to read the book itself? If you cannot find time to read the work, you are better off with the notes than with no information at all. However, these notes do not get at the real flavor of the original classic. So you are to an extent depriving yourself of your education. Although you will learn better if you read and make notes yourself, published notes often are useful for review when you have not had time to make notes. The same applies to other kinds of review books as well.

Non-classics.　If the book is not yet a classic, and it is not likely to be if the author is still alive, you will have to deal with the author's ideas without the assistance of an editor. It is regrettable that some authors prefer difficult to easy words and often use very long, involved sentences. Sometimes, they even make up their own vocabulary. If the author does much of this, it is wise to resort once more to 3 x 5 cards, arranged alphabetically. Take the author's definition down when he gives it; then, when he uses it later, you won't have to hunt back through the book to find out what it was he meant. You will have the definition available.

Notes on outside readings.   Taking notes on outside readings is different from taking notes from textbooks. Read a whole chapter or section at a time and then summarize it briefly (no more than a paragraph or two). The summary should state the main ideas and relate these to the central concept of the work. If the book is a classic, you will know what the main concept is from having read the editor's introduction. If there is no editor's introduction, the author's introductory chapter may serve the same purpose. But it may not, too. Sometimes, the main idea will be too difficult to understand from the introduction alone. (This could be the author's fault, not yours, but you will still have to deal with it.) If you cannot understand the main thrust of the book from the introductory chapter, try reading the last chapter where the author gives his conclusions. That may help. Occasionally, it may be necessary to seek help from your teacher or from another student.

When you have finished summarizing the chapters, sum up the main ideas and give your own opinion about the work. Back this up with as much solid evidence and/or respected opinion as you can think of. If you are familiar with another work dealing with the same concept, compare the two. Try to keep your summary to a paragraph and your critique to a couple of paragraphs. Commenting on the book will help to anchor it in your mind; it will also be useful should your teacher include an exam question about that book.

If an outside reading should prove to be beyond your reading skill even when you work at it, see if you can substitute another book from the teacher's list. Frequently teachers offer some options with respect to outside reading.

IMPROVING YOUR READING

The more you read the more your reading skill will improve. However, a conscious effort to improve will speed up the process. For one thing, you should try to improve your vocabulary. The best way to do this is to always have a dictionary at hand to look up any unfamiliar words you come across and to write them on 3 x 5 cards, putting the definitions on the back. Keep the cards with you and study them from time to time. Even the seconds afforded by a stoplight is enough to review the meaning of one or two words in your own language.

Try also to increase your reading speed. From time to time, consciously push yourself to read a little faster. Occasionally time yourself to see how fast you can read a given number of pages.

Practice skimming, that is, reading rapidly through a chapter to get the most important ideas. Or skim just to find the author's view of a particular idea or person.

Practicing these reading skills will not only make you a better reader; you will also become a better studier and, where time is a factor, a better test-taker. Finally, you will become a speedier researcher, and the task of writing research papers will be easier.

ADVANTAGES OF BEING A
GOOD READER

Reading is the key to education, and being a good reader is the mark of an educated person. Your years in college should greatly improve your ability to read, both in speed and understanding.

As much as anything else, it is the college graduate's greater reading ability which gives him or her an advantage over the high school graduate in the job market. So important is the skill to read and absorb great quantities of material that businessmen and politicians often take speed-reading courses so they can get through the large volume of reading matter that piles up on their desks. Such courses are helpful, but they should not be necessary for you if you make an effort to improve your reading throughout your college career. In the process of learning to be a successful college student, you should learn to read well.

CHAPTER VI

Getting the Most
Out of Classes

The student who pays $100 a credit for his courses (not an extraordinarily high price these days) is paying more than $7.00 an hour for class time, either personally or through his parents. It is up to the student how he or she uses this time. Students are presumed to be sufficiently adult to go to the classes they have paid for; it is a rare college these days which enforces class attendance. Class-cutting is, therefore, extremely common, especially on Friday afternoons.

GOING TO CLASS PAYS OFF

Going to class pays off in good grades, and students who want good grades go to them. Other things being equal, the student who goes to classes regularly will be a full grade higher in his final evaluation than one who cuts frequently. Obviously, there must be some learning benefits in going to class.

One advantage of going to class is getting to know the teacher well. Every teacher has expectations, peculiarities, prejudices, and attitudes with which it pays a student to be familiar. Most teachers make a genuine effort to be fair to students and not penalize them for their views, but teachers are prisoners of their own thinking as are the rest of us. By listening in class to the asides, the little jokes, the contemptuous remarks, a student can get a pretty clear idea of what will meet with a teacher's approval and what will not. One of the characteristics of most teachers is that they resent deliberate absence from class; so if you are ill or are forced to cut for some necessary reason, call up and explain.

Second, the student who goes to class becomes known by the teacher, and, usually, this is to the student's advantage. Don't be too shy to talk over some of your problems with the teacher. Not only may you get some good advice, but the teacher will have a better understanding of you and will be more likely to make allowances for your weaknesses. Furthermore, class participation wins brownie points. If you speak up in class and offer information or opinions, you are likely to be remembered as a wide-awake student even if some of your information is wrong. A record of good attendance will be counted for you when grades are made up, especially if you are on the borderline between two grades. If your grade falls between a B and an A, you are much more likely to get the latter if you have been in class regularly and have been an active participant.

Third, the student who attends class regularly gets to know the other students, and they can be a valuable resource. If you are absent owing to illness, another student whom you know will probably be willing to lend you the notes or to run off a copy for you. If another student takes better notes than you do, you may be able to borrow and run off the entire course for yourself. A student who has a better background than you have can often explain to you concepts and ideas which you find difficult. Some students are willing to voluntarily tutor other students whom they know and like. Finally, other students are often good resources when you are reviewing for exams. So go to class and get the advantage of knowing the other students. Conversely, if you know the other students, you are more likely to attend.

Finally, classes are held for the purpose of imparting and clarifying information. By not going to class, you may be missing some critical information that will turn up on the final examination.

Teachers are justified in including on an examination any information covered either in the readings or in class.

USING CLASS TIME
EFFECTIVELY

Going to class is better than not going to class even if you are only half there. But being all there is better yet because it is important to remember what goes on in class. Talking to neighbors in class not only makes you inattentive, it distracts others and annoys the teacher. Keep it to a minimum.

Assuming that you are wide awake and not talking to your neighbors, how can you make the most of your class time? In this book, we will first distinguish between "regular" classes and seminars. A seminar is a small group (usually fewer than 10 people) in which each student is expected to do research and make a presentation to the class. Seminars are more common at the graduate level than the undergraduate level. However, quite a few schools do offer seminars to undergraduate students. A regular class is anything other than a seminar, and it may vary from a lecture with up to 500 students to a relatively small (15 to 20 people) discussion-type group. Since regular classes are the kind undergraduates experience most frequently, we will deal with them first.

Regular Classes

Generally speaking, the information offered in a regular class will be one of four types: (1) New information not available in any of the readings, (2) clarification of the text, (3) discussions designed to give the students new insights, and (4) pre-examination review.

New information not available in the text is usually offered in a straight lecture. There will be relatively few questions from teacher to students, and the teacher may talk fairly fast. In this case, the problem will be to get the major ideas down in your notes since there will not be time to write out all the details. If the teacher puts an outline on the blackboard while lecturing, taking notes will be easy. Just follow what is on the board and fill in the gaps where you feel more detail is needed for you to remember or to understand. If the teacher just zips along a mile a minute, you may get lost and not see the organization of the lecture at all. Here is where contact with other students can be helpful. It's a good idea, when a teacher is a zipper, to plan for regular meetings with other students in the class—especially the good note takers—to share notes and discuss what was said. Often this will clarify ideas or bring to your attention facts and concepts which you had overlooked in your rush.

Clarification of what is in a textbook is usually the style only where the text is particularly difficult. It may take the form of either a straight lecture or a combination of lecture and question and answer. Notes for this kind of class are probably easiest to take if you bring the book to class with you and follow the text while the teacher is talking. This will give you a chance to ask questions about parts of the reading which proved difficult for you. Write down, giving the page reference of the book, interpretations which clarify it. Make notes also on those parts of the text which the teacher emphasized. This will give you a clue to what may be on the examination.

The discussion aimed at giving students new insights is quite different from either of the above. Usually, a single major concept will be dealt with, and students will be encouraged by means of questions directed at the class to develop their own ideas concerning this concept. The emphasis here is on participation. Get involved, raise questions, express your own views. Note taking in this classroom environment may be difficult, so put your notebooks aside for the time being. Chances are the teacher will sum up the important points before the class comes to an end. Then is the time to take down what is said and written on the blackboard. Again, sitting down with other students from the class after it is over may be a good way to bring out the major points in the discussion.

Most teachers will present a mixture of these classroom styles. Furthermore, the same teacher will vary the style according to the content of the course and the difficulty of the readings. Skills courses, especially, will need emphasis on clarification while content courses may lean heavily on new information.

What if the teacher turns you off or bores you, and you just don't want to go to class? This is bound to happen sometimes. You are certain to like some teachers less than others, and boredom is one of the facts of life. The more you participate, however, the less bored you will be. (Don't try to hog the whole show, however. Other students resent it, and so do teachers.) It is up to you to motivate yourself to a considerable degree. Teachers owe you clarity and an attempt to help you understand; they do not owe you entertainment.

What if the teacher's lectures are over your head? By over your head, I mean where you are so lost that you cannot ask an intelligent question because you don't know what question to ask. This is a serious problem, but how serious depends on how frequently it happens. If it happens only occasionally, it may be because you missed something said in a previous class or did not understand fully something in the readings. Often, it is the result of not having a good vocabulary either in English generally or in the teacher's discipline. don't be timid; ask a question. Say something like, "I'm sorry, but I don't understand the idea," or, "I'm lost, please explain." The chances are good that, if you don't understand, someone else in the class is also in the dark. If the answer is conceptual, get the clarification of the concept into your class notes. If the answer is definitional, get it on a 3 x 5 card.

If the class is so large that there is no opportunity to ask questions, other students may be your only resource. However, most courses based on large lectures will have scheduled a period once a week where the students meet in small groups and discuss the materials of the course. Here is your opportunity to ask questions about the lectures and the readings. It is wise, if you are enrolled in a course featuring such a lecture-discussion combination, to write down immediately after each lecture the questions which you will want to raise at the next discussion. If you don't write them down, you will surely forget them. Some of these questions may be answered by your reading or discussions with other students before you get to your discussion group; however, the very process of thinking through a lecture immediately after it is over will help you to remember it.

One thing is important; do not get into the habit of cutting discussion groups. It is an interesting phenomenon that students in lecture courses, when asked how they feel about discussion groups, always emphasize their importance; nevertheless, the discussion group is the class which is most frequently cut. Possibly this is due to the students' awareness that new information will not be offered since the discussion group is devoted to examination and clarification of ideas developed in the lectures and readings. The discussion group is your opportunity to get better understanding, to participate and expand your capacity to think and, not unimportant, to exchange ideas with faculty members whose minds are more mature than your own owing to their greater educational background.

If you often find yourself in the dark concerning the teacher's meaning, the problem deserves further analysis. Check with other students in the class to see if they, too, are lost. If so, the problem may be with the professor. Form a delegation and go talk to him or her about the problem. (Be tactful; teachers are more sensitive than most students realize.) If that teacher has just come to the school, he or she may be accustomed to a level of student-body which is more highly educated than that of your alma mater. Recent graduate students frequently have this problem; they are accustomed to the company of other graduate students and may not realize how difficult their vocabulary is for the person who is less experienced in the field. If the teacher is an open-minded person, he or sure will appreciate your information and will probably do better in the future.

If you are alone in the dark, you will have to take some other kind of action. Discuss your problem with the teacher or discussion leader. If you are not too far lost or if your confusion results simply from being behind, you may be able to save the situation by taking an incomplete and making the course up the next semester. However, you may have been mistakenly advised into a course for which you are not adequately prepared. In that case, it is probably wise to drop the course even at the cost of losing some of the tuition. Even if the fault is that of your advisor, the college will not take the responsibility. You are the final decision-maker regarding your own program. One caution—if you are having real problems with a course, do not wait too long to take some action; there is often a time limit after which you cannot withdraw without penalty.

Going to class offers you an opportunity to clarify the course requirements. Teachers often have different standards respecting, for example, the requirements for a research paper. Some may be quite permissive about footnoting, spelling, and so on; others will be strict. You are wise to get your teacher's view on the adequacy of a topic. Take a few minutes after class to ask: "Is *Andrew Jackson and the Bank of the United States* a good topic for a term paper?" "Have you any suggestions concerning sources for my paper?" "What kinds of things must be footnoted?" Although teachers are expected to have office hours when they can confer with students, they are sometimes hard to get hold of, and right after class may be your best opportunity.

Classes are an essential part of your education. If you cut them frequently, you are throwing away your money or that of your parents. The result will almost certainly be a lowered grade.

Seminars

Since a seminar is a small class where each student is expected to report to the class on research done independently, your grade will be based very heavily on your participation. Information in student reports will be an integral part of the total course. Therefore, not only courtesy demands that you hear other students' reports as they are expected to hear yours. Furthermore, your questions about the other students' methods of doing their research and your criticisms of their information are part of your learning process.

When you are the student giving a report, it is essential that you be prepared, that your report be complete and intelligible and that you are ready to answer questions about it from other students and from the teacher. Since most seminar reports are essentially research papers which are read in class, more information concerning successful reports will be found in the chapter devoted to research papers.

It is to be hoped that this chapter has convinced you of the undesirability of wasting your educational investment by cutting class. However, the temptations will be great at times. Resisting temptation and going to class regularly are, like other study habits, largely a matter of routine. Mature individuals who value their education will develop the habit of good class attendance.

CHAPTER VII

Writing Research Papers

A common type of assignment in college is the research paper. A student must select a topic, do research on some aspect of it and write up the results, all more or less independently. Unfortunately, very few students have had any experience at the high school level with the kind of research needed to do an adequate research paper. In this chapter, we will attempt to give you some general rules which will help you to write good research papers.

MAKE IT YOUR OWN

The most important characteristic of a good research paper is that it be your own. Although this means, of course, that the paper must not be bought or borrowed from someone else, it goes beyond that. It means that the paper must be original. This does not mean that you cannot borrow information and ideas from other sources; a paper may be based entirely on information gathered in a library. What it does mean is that in borrowing data and ideas from others you must put them together in a way which is uniquely your own. In short, what you must not do is "lift."

What is a lift? Most students recognize that outright copying of someone else's work without giving credit is plagiarism and dishonest. What many students do not realize is that paraphrasing large sections of another person's book or article, even with a reference giving credit to the original author, is lifting and is unacceptable. Students who lean too heavily on the work of one, two or even a few authors often make this mistake. A teacher is justified in giving an F for a lifted paper, because essentially it is not the student's own work.

In order to avoid bought, borrowed or lifted papers, some teachers assign topics. In this way, they become very familiar with the literature in a field and can quickly detect a dishonest paper. Other teachers prefer to have the student pick a topic related to the course because they feel that learning to pick a topic is part of learning to write an original paper.

PICKING A TOPIC

Many students hate to pick a topic. Yet picking a good topic is the first step in writing a good paper. Choosing a topic that is just right for you as an individual is essential to writing a paper which is uniquely your own. Essentially, it is an exercise in imagination, and, therefore, it usually requires a good deal of thinking. The topic must be well-selected to meet the requirements set for it.

Subject Matter of the Course

Few teachers will accept a paper which is not fairly closely related to the subject matter of the course. Therefore, you must find a topic that fits in well with the course content. One way to go about this is to study the table of contents of your textbook until you find a general subject which is of interest to you. Then skim through the chapter on that subject until you find what subdivision or sub-subdivision you would like to know more about. Although this will usually be too broad for a research paper, some aspect of it will make a suitable topic since it is bound to be related to the subject of the course.

The media are often a good source of topics.[1] So are class lectures. Some students have a pet subject which they like to explore from many angles. Any of these are useful sources for picking a topic.

Required Length of the Paper

Most writing assignments are expressed in terms of length. However, when a teacher asks you to write a paper of 2000 to 2500 words or of 10 to 15 pages,[2] it is not his or her intention to limit you to exactly that amount but merely to suggest about how long a paper must be to meet the course requirement. Students often take the word requirement as the most important requirement of all and diligently pad away, counting as they go. *This is not the way to write a paper.* The idea is to make an intelligent guess as to what topic will fit the word requirement fairly well and then write the paper to cover the topic adequately without worrying too much about the word count. Ninety-nine times out of a hundred, the topic chosen by a student to meet a term paper requirement is much too broad to be covered in the number of words specified and must be reduced in scope.

Your Own Interests

Writing a paper is dull work if you are not interested in the topic, but it can be a very satisfying kind of assignment if you are interested. So try to find a topic which you care about.

Develop a Point of View

A topic is most successful if it represents a point of view which is uniquely your own. One way to go about this is, after you have selected your topic and narrowed it down to what seems

---

[1] Newspapers, magazines, radio and television constitute the *media.* The word is plural. The singular is *medium.*

[2] An 8½-by-11-inch double-spaced typewritten page has about 250 words. Thus a 2500-word paper would be about 10 pages.

to be manageable size, ask yourself questions about it. This requires a good deal of thinking, and it is a good idea to write down your questions as you go along. Suppose that, for a course in economics, you have decided to write about the use of nuclear power to produce electricity. Some of the following questions might occur to you. "Will radioactive wastes poison the oceans?" "What really happened at Three Mile Island nuclear plant?" "Is a nuclear plant really efficient economically?" "Could a meltdown of the nuclear core lead to a disastrous explosion?" When you have a question to which you would like to find the answer, you are probably ready to go ahead and work on your paper.

However, it is wise at this point to check your topic with your teacher. He or she can give you an idea not only of its appropriateness but also whether it is too broad to cover in the length required. The teacher may also make suggestions as to narrowing it down and will probably have some ideas about sources of information.

Preliminary Library Research

If you or your teacher has any doubts about the availability of information on your topic, you will be wise to browse through the library to see what is available. Consult the card cataglog and talk to the reference librarians. Write down the names of some places in the library where you may find information, but do not spend a lot of time on research yet. If your topic looks hopelessly void of sources of information, discard it and choose another. Usually, material will be available and you can begin to plan the writing of your paper.

PLANNING HOW TO WRITE
ABOUT YOUR TOPIC

Once you plan to go ahead with a topic, don't just pull out all the books you can find relating to it. That wastes time. You must pin your topic down by writing a topic statement and a preliminary outline.

The Topic Statement

To write a topic statement, write the question you plan to research in the form of a statement. Suppose the question you want to answer is: "Could a meltdown lead to a disastrous explosion?" Although this question seems pretty specific, in fact most of the terms in it must be carefully limited before your start. You might come up with: "This paper will investigate the probability that a meltdown of the nuclear core of a reactor could result in an explosion which would cause death or illness to a large number of people." Although there are still some ambiguities in this statement, it is much more specific than the original question. The advantage of such a topic statement is that it clarifies for you what you are looking for and thereby cuts down on your research.

The Preliminary Outline

Once you have your topic statement, it is helpful to prepare a preliminary outline. Many students say that they cannot do an outline until they have done all the reading. Not so—by thinking about your paper you can do a very satisfactory preliminary outline, often after doing only a minimum of reading or sometimes no reading at all.

In the first place, all papers have three parts, a beginning, a middle and an end. The beginning is your introduction. When writing a research paper, the introduction will state what it is you are going to investigate and will clarify any ambiguous terms you are using. The middle of your paper will be devoted to the evidence, mostly facts and opinions taken from the writings of others.[3] The end will be your conclusion; here you will sum up your evidence and state your decision concerning the solution to the problem which was stated in your introduction. These sec-

---

[3] Using the work of others does not, of course, preclude your doing some original research of your own, such as circulating a questionnaire, doing an experiment, and the like.

tions could be the major divisions—I, II and III—of your paper. If you already know that your evidence will break down into several major sections so that the middle of your paper will have two or more parts, you would have more than three major subdivisions. In order to do a preliminary outline, you must decide what breakdown seems most logical to you at the outset.

Often you will be able to subdivide your paper even further. Suppose, as a result of something your teacher has said, you decide to investigate the Hamilton-Burr duel. Your topic statement says: "This paper will attempt to reconstruct the actual events of the duel between Alexander Hamilton and Aaron Burr." Your preliminary outline might be somewhat as follows:

I. Introduction: Statement of the problem
   A. The generally accepted account of the events of the duel
   B. Reasons for thinking the account may be incorrect
   C. Statement of purpose: to reconstruct the events of the duel itself
II. Evidence
   A. Analysis of available sources of information
   B. Differences among these sources
      1. Pro-Hamilton sources
      2. Pro-Burr sources
   C. Evaluation of the reliability of the sources
III. Summary and conclusion

Most of what is in that outline is a result of thought. True, the existence of a possible difference of opinion over the events of the duel would have had to come from either a lecture or preliminary reading. The rest, however, results entirely from thinking: "What is it I want to focus on?" "What kinds of information are likely to be available?" "What are the natural subdivisions of this subject?"

The advantages of doing a topic statement and tentative outline before even starting on the research are that: (1) The outline will serve as a guide to your reading; and (2) topic statement and outline make the paper your own; it will not become just a rehash of someone else's work.

You are, of course, not permanently bound by your preliminary outline. Most outlines change considerably as the research progresses. Your topic statement, on the other hand, should not be changed except for good reason, because that would change your topic.

DOING RESEARCH

Several problems face students in doing research for a paper: finding information, evaluating it and taking notes on it.

Finding Information

How to find information for a paper for a particular course is beyond the scope of this book. Each discipline has its own sources. Your college library may have published a bibliography of the major sources in the field you are researching; pick one up. The following suggestions may also be of help. Your course textbook may be a good source of information on the general topic of your research paper. Look at the footnotes and/or the bibliography. You will find listed what are probably the "best," that is to say, the accepted, references there. Encyclopedias may also be good sources of general information; there are many specialized encyclopedias so browse about in that section of the reference room or ask the reference librarian. The library card catalog subject section may also provide you with books. Indexes, of which there are a large number, both general and specific to various fields, can lead you to books and articles on your topic. Footnote references in the books and articles you read will prove to be a very valuable source. The reference librarian can help you most of all. When in doubt, ask him or her. In addition, there are many published guides to research sources. Finally, your teacher will probably be willing to make some suggestions.

Whenever you find a reference to a book or an article which you think will be helpful, write it down on a 3 x 5 card. Be sure to put it in correct bibliographical form. For example:

Fish, Carl Russell. *The Civil Service and the Patronage.* (Harvard Historical Studies, XI). New York: Longman's Green and Co., 1905.

Book covers 1789 to 1901. Very good.

AH 5 (2d fl.) Harvard Guide,
 R 33   p. 152

You will notice that the card contains the author, title, series (if any), the place of publication, the publisher and the date of publication, all in proper bibliographical style. It also contains the "call" number of the book on the lower left, that is, the number by which it is identified in your library and which will enable you to find it. Next to the call number is given the floor of the "stack."[4] In the lower right-hand corner is the name of the source of the reference with the page number; if your library does not have the book (or article), you will need that in order to have it borrowed for you. In the middle of the card is your comment on the value of this item to your research. Even if your comment is "no good," keep the card and place it in alphabetical order with the cards for each of the other books and articles you come across. Having

---

[4] A stack is where a book is shelved.

a rejected item in your bibliographical file will prevent you from looking it up again should you come across it and not remember having seen it.

When you finish your paper, you will take from your bibliographical file all those references for which you have foot- or endnotes (all the books and articles "cited"). Then you will type your bibliography from that set. Remember that an adequate bibliography should include a good selection of both books and articles.

Evaluating Sources

Not all printed materials are of equal value. It is the task of the researcher to decide which of the sources he consults are reliable and which are questionable. Although the undergraduate researcher is not expected to have the expertise in source evaluation of a fully-trained scholar, he or she is still expected to use good judgment in the selection of sources.

Obviously, what sources you use depends on the topic of your paper. It is much beyond the scope of this book to offer criteria for evaluating all the possible materials a college student might use in writing undergraduate term papers. However, a few rules of thumb may be helpful:

1. References given in your textbooks are likely to be to authoritative sources.
2. Articles which appear in academic journals are usually reviewed by experts in the field called referees.
3. Articles found in good general or specialized encyclopedias are by authorities and are reviewed for accuracy by the editorial staff.
4. Articles in the generally accepted national popular journals (such as *Time, Newsweek, Fortune, Business Week,* etc.) are written by people who are qualified writers, but they are not reviewed by referees.
5. Articles in the *New York Times* or other "respectable" news-

papers are written by highly-paid well-qualified journalists, but news stories are often written under pressure and from limited sources so that their accuracy may sometimes suffer.

6. Articles written in journals which cater to superstition and sensationalism (such as the *National Enquirer*) are highly suspect with respect to accuracy.

7. Most documents produced by government agencies are written by qualified researchers.

8. Government documents written by political units of government (such as Congress or a state legislature) should be used cautiously because they are sometimes edited for political reasons—the *Congressional Record,* for example).

9. Pamphlets devoted to particular political, religious or ethnic causes are likely to be biased.

In writing research papers, you will get a better grade if you have used good judgment in selecting your sources. If you are in doubt about the use of a particular source, ask the teacher.

Reading

Research reading is very different from reading a text. In reading a book as part of the research for a paper, you almost never read all of it. Instead, look up your topic in the index and turn to the indicated pages. You will probably have to use imagination to think of terms under which your topic might be listed because indexing systems differ. If you find something worthwhile, note it down.

To make sure that an article is on your topic, read the abstract (short summary) if there is one. To find the information you want, it will probably be necessary to go through an article in its entirety. However, you should learn to skim, using headings as guides, until you find material which relates to your topic. Then, of course, you must read slowly and carefully and take notes.

Note Taking

Note taking is of three kinds: summary notes, verbatim notes, and paraphrases. Notes can be done in two ways, on 3 x 5 (or larger) cards or on the duplicating machines, which all libraries now have. When taking notes on cards, always use cards of the same size so they can be filed in a box, and limit yourself to one idea to a card. Be sure to write in the upper right-hand corner the name of the author and the pages from which the note is taken. It is unnecessary to take down all the bibliographical information because you need only enough to refer you back to the bibliographical card. However, if you are using more than one book by the same author, you must also include on your note card enough of the title to indicate which book you are using.

Because taking notes on cards is time consuming, many students prefer to take most of their notes on the duplicating machines. However, this is expensive; you will have to make your own decision about whether hand-written or duplicated notes are the best for you in each case. Most people end up with some of each. If you use the machine, be sure to make a note of the source of the material on each page you duplicate. You must do this at the time you make the duplication; otherwise, you are sure to forget where you got the material, and you may be unable to find it again. If so, since you are responsible for noting every bit of information or opinion taken from another source, you cannot use the information from that duplicated page. It is also a good idea, after taking notes by machine, to go over the pages and underline the parts which you had in mind when you did the duplication. This will save you much later rereading.

When taking notes you must decide whether to summarize, to paraphrase or to take the item verbatim (exactly as written). Summary notes sum up several pages of background material in a small space. They should be in your own words, preferably in full sentences. Paraphrased notes take down all the facts or opinions respecting a particular item but put them in different words. it is important when paraphrasing to use your own words entirely and not simply change a word here or there. If you change only an occasional word and then use that item in your paper as it is written in your notes, you will be guilty of plagiarism. Paraphrasing is best used only when turning technical language of the original source into layman's language. Often it is better, if the section is not too long, to copy it verbatim and do the paraphrasing in your paper. Summary and paraphrased notes, obviously, must go on cards.

Verbatim notes can be taken either on cards or by machine. It is important to use quotation marks around everything which is taken from the original source onto a card. If you leave something out of the verbatim note, you must use an ellipsis. An ellipsis (plural, ellipses) consists of three dots with spaces between them. If the ellipsis includes the end of a sentence, add an extra dot to represent the period. If an entire paragraph is omitted, begin the next paragraph with three dots. The use of ellipses is illustrated below:

> "The language is perpetually in flux: it is a living stream, . . . losing old forms in the backwaters of time. . . . No idiom is taboo, no accent forbidden. . . .
>
> ". . . Style takes its final shape more from attitudes of mind than from principles of composition. . . ."[5]

In the quotation above, quotation marks are used at the beginning and end as they should be on a note card to indicate when an item is a direct quotation. (In a block quotation in a paper, quotation marks are omitted.) The first sentence has several words omitted as indicated by the three dots between "stream" and "losing." At the end of the first sentence, a sentence or more is omitted as indicated by four dots. Beginning the next paragraph,

---

[5] William Strunk, Jr. and E. B. White, *The Elements of Style,* 2d ed. (New York: Macmillan, 1972), pp. 76–77.

the three-dot ellipsis shows that a paragraph has been omitted. In taking verbatim notes, it is very important to observe these technicalities so that when you use the note in your paper, you will know exactly where words have been omitted.

WRITING YOUR PAPER

Writing a paper consists basically of three steps: (1) Expanding the preliminary outline into the final outline, (2) writing the first draft of the paper, and (3) revising the first draft into the second draft.

Expanding the Outline

As you begin to do research, the preliminary outline will grow and possibly change radically. The three major subdivisions will remain the same, but the breakdown of the middle, usually II, may grow into several main points. Since the preliminary outline was only a general guide, you may find as you get into the information that the breakdown you selected originally is not the most feasible, and you may have to change it.

As you read more, you will be able to subdivide your outline into smaller and smaller parts. When you review your notes, you should write on the cards or duplication sheets where that information fits into the outline. When you have classified all of your notes, you may find that there are gaps in your information. Some part of your outline which fits in logically has no evidence to support it. In that case, you must return to the library to see if you can find information to fill the gap. Sometimes, of course, the information will not be available. What do you do? Wherever there is a gap in information which will be obvious to the reader, you must explain, either in the text or in a footnote, whichever is more suitable, that the information was not available.

Writing the First Draft

When you have completed your outline, you are ready to write. Sort your note cards and duplicator printouts in the order of your outline and begin to write. Be sure that the information is completely in your own words except where you are quoting. Do not quote too frequently. The paper, remember, is your own, not just a series of lifts from other authors. It is a good rule that you should use a quotation only if what is quoted is so well stated and fits into your own plan for your paper so well that it cannot be improved upon; this is rare. As you go along, insert numbers for foot- and endnotes. Keep in mind that any fact or opinion which comes from a source other than your own brain must be given a note *whether or not it is directly quoted.* The only exception is common knowledge. People do not always agree on what constitutes common knowledge, but it is probably wise for undergraduate students to err on the side of too many, rather than too few, footnotes. One way to keep tract of footnotes is to insert the source and page in brackets after the material which requires the note. Then, when you type the final draft, you can put this reference into proper form.

When you have finished the first draft from beginning to end, retype any pages which are difficult to read because of inserts or lines drawn to show a change in the order of words or sentences. If the paper is for a social science or science course, divide it into sections with headings to correspond to the main sections in your outline (as this book is written). If the paper is very long, you may also need chapters. Humanities teachers may prefer that you not use headings for the subdivisions of your paper. It is wise to check this point with your teacher.

Any paper which has many specialized words in it will also need a glossary at the end. A good research paper should be readable by any educated person. Therefore, using highly-specialized words without defining them is undesirable. In expository writing, the aim should be for clarity.

After your paper is in readable form, put it away, preferably for several days or a week. This is to let it cool for a while so that errors in spelling, punctuation, syntax and diction, as well as gaps in thinking or lack of clarity, will be obvious to you. When as much time as you can afford has elapsed, take the paper out and revise it. Eliminate errors and smooth out the style. While you are working, be sure to have available a dictionary, a grammar book and, if you need it, a thesaurus.[6] Other than the suggestions already made, this book will make no attempt to improve your writing style. Numerous books are available to help you with your prose. If you have real problems with English, you should take a corrective writing course as soon as possible.

The Final Draft

When you have finished correcting your first draft, type the final draft, inserting the notes. Notes may be placed either at the foot of the page (footnotes) or at the end of the paper (end-notes). Check with your teacher concerning the form of the notes. Different disciplines have different preferred noting formats.[7]

Let your final draft rest for a day, also. Then reread it very carefully to correct any errors. If the errors on a page are few, it will be acceptable to most teachers if you correct them in ink. After you have finished your corrections, look through the pages again. Are there any which look so bad that they should be re-typed? Are the pages all numbered consecutively in the upper right-hand corner? If your paper has illustrations, does each one have a note giving credit for the source of the information? If the paper is lengthy and subdivided with headings, a table of contents may be needed. If there are several illustrations, a list of illustrations should be typed on a separate page to follow the table of contents.

---

[6] A thesaurus is the opposite of a dictionary. One starts with the meaning he has in mind and uses the thesaurus to find an appropriate word or phrase to express it.

[7] English grammar books designed for college use always have a discussion of correct footnoting.

When you are satisfied with the paper, type a cover sheet with the name of the paper in capitals centered about halfway down, the word "by" centered two lines below and your name centered two lines below that. In the lower right-hand corner of the cover sheet, type the name of the course, the name of the teacher and the date.

Now take the entire paper to the duplicating machine and run off a copy. It is important to have in your files a copy of every paper you have written. Teachers occasionally lose papers, or they do not return them after they are graded. If the paper receives a good grade, you should always have a copy to submit in case of necessity. Sometimes a paper can be used as the basis for the waiver of a required course. Not infrequently, a graduate or professional school will want to see a sample of your papers before deciding whether to admit you to its program. An employer who is looking for someone who can write well may want to see one or two papers as a sample of your writing ability. So you can see that it is essential to keep a copy; a duplicated copy is usually better in appearance than a carbon copy, although a carbon will do if you cannot afford the duplication costs.

Finally, hand in the paper, making sure that your instructor gets the original, not the duplicate.

SOME GENERAL
SUGGESTIONS

In addition to these step-by-step suggestions, a few general rules may be helpful. Always start papers early in the term. They usually take more time to complete than you expect. The paper which is written off the top of the head at the last minute rarely gets a good grade. Besides, you may need to borrow material from a library other than the college library or ask the college library to borrow for you, and these things take time.

If you find it hard to get started working and to keep at the job of writing a paper, it will be useful to set yourself a time schedule. For example:

Finish: Topic statement, preliminary outline by Oct. 10.
Research by Nov. 15.
First draft by Dec. 15.
Final draft by Christmas vacation.

The deadlines in your paper-writing schedule should be incorporated in your weekly study plans. If you have difficulty getting started working on your paper after you have been away from it for a time, read over what you have done. That will start your brain working on it.

After a paper is returned to you, always review your teacher's comments. These may be helpful in writing later papers.

THE VALUE OF WRITING PAPERS

Writing papers is among the most valuable educational experiences of a college education. Finding information to develop an idea of your own and putting that information in a form to communicate to others is a mind-stretching and psychologically satisfying experience. Furthermore, it involves a set of skills which are essential in many professions and in high demand in the business world.

CHAPTER VIII

Studying for Examinations

Probably the greatest mental hurdle which students face is an examination. Yet the student who has studied well all during the term rarely has much to worry about. This discussion assumes that you have been studying and keeping up with your courses and need merely to review in order to take your examinations with confidence.[1]

A few suggestions may help to make your review most effective. All reviewing for an examination should not be done the night before the examination. Ideally, it should be done at intervals throughout the semester. Since few people do that, the next best thing is to start at least two weeks before the examination. Try to get through all the material (class notes and reading notes or underlinings) at least three times. The more often you repeat a learning experience, the more likely you are to remember it. As you review, try to pick out what you think will be emphasized on the examination.

---

[1] There is no good way to cram for examinations. Cramming is probably better than not studying at all, but it rarely results in a good grade.

LEARNING WHAT YOU CAN
IN ADVANCE

Since your method of review will vary somewhat with the type of examination your teacher gives, it will pay you to learn as much as possible about the exam in advance. The most reliable source of information will be the teacher, who will usually be willing to give you a good deal of help, short of telling you the actual questions. Another possible source of information is students who have taken the same course in previous years with the same teacher.

Type of Examination

It is a rare teacher who will not tell whether the exam will be objective or essay or a combination of both.

Objective examination. Objective examinations, so-called, are those in which a statement is made or a question asked; the student is expected to select from a choice of answers the one which best completes the statement or best answers the question. Such answers are of two basic types: true-false and multiple-choice. The true-false test is considered quite easy since the student has a fifty-fifty chance of getting the right answer. For this reason, many college teachers avoid them. The multiple-choice test usually offers four or five possible answers to each question. The correct answer may involve either recall of facts or opinions or a correct inference from information given in the stem of the question. Following is an example of an objective question requiring recall of information:

> In which of the years listed below did Columbus discover America?
> A. 1066
> B. 1492
> C. 1776
> D. 1507

Obviously, the answer is B, 1492.

Following is an example of an objective question requiring inference from information given in the stem:

> Since a congressman must be constantly meeting people both while campaigning and while in office, it is probable that few congressmen suffer from:
> A. Shyness
> B. Greediness
> C. Dilatoriness
> D. Over-assertiveness

Again, the answer is obvious; A, shyness. Needless to say, your college test will not be this easy.

Good objective tests are difficult to write because the questions or statements and the possible answers must be carefully phrased if they are to be a fair test of the material—neither too much devoted to minor points nor so vague as to be misleading— and not give away the answers to other questions. Writing them, therefore, takes a good deal of time, and the teacher is unlikely to give an objective exam if the class is small. The objective test is, however, quick to grade, guaranteed against favoritism and has the advantage that it can cover factual material in more detail than can a subjective exam.

Subjective examinations. Subjective examinations are also known as essay examinations. These may consist of several short essay questions, worth 5 or 10 points each, and one or two longer ones, worth from 25 to 50 points each, or any combination the teacher thinks suitable. The following might be a test for an American History course:

> Part I: For 10 points each discuss *five* of the following:
> A. Manifest destiny
> B. Salutary neglect
> C. Dollar diplomacy

D. The Fourteen Points

E. The Four Freedoms

F. The Monroe Doctrine

Part II: For 25 points each discuss *two* of the following:

A. The major political and economic tenets of Jacksonianism

B. A comparison and contrast of the populists and progressives

C. An analysis of changes brought about by the New Deal

Note that, as above, an essay test may offer the student a choice of questions to answer. While this gives the student a chance to omit a question to which he or she does not know the answer, it also allows the teacher to maintain a strict standard of grading. Essay tests given at the undergraduate level rarely call for very long essays such as a single essay worth 100 percent of the possible examination score.[2]

Essay examinations take a long time to grade, and teachers are unlikely to offer them to large classes. They have the advantage of testing students' ability to organize their thinking and to express themselves respecting the concepts of a course. On the other hand, it is difficult to cover a great many facts in an essay format.

Specialized types of tests, such as the take-home examination or the "prepared question," will not be discussed here; teachers who offer them usually spend considerable time explaining how the students should go about them.

Grading Procedure

Although the procedure the teacher uses to grade examinations should make relatively little difference to the way you review, it is important to how you take the test. So it pays to learn how the examination is going to be graded.

---

[2] The single-question essay examination is fairly common at the graduate level.

Scoring of objective examination question. In scoring objective examinations, most teachers simply add the number of wrong answers to the number of omitted questions, multiply by the value of each question and subtract the result from 100 to obtain the student's score. However, this means that on a true-false test, a person has a fifty-fifty chance to get the right answer even if he knows nothing. On a four-answer multiple-choice test, the chance is 25 percent (one out of four) and, on a five-answer multiple-choice test, the chance is 20 percent (one out of five). Therefore, a teacher may subtract the number wrong from the number right or some part of the number wrong from the number right in order to eliminate this chance. It is important for you to know how the teacher scores multiple-choice tests.

Scoring of essay examination questions. Teachers' methods of scoring essay questions probably differ more than do their methods of scoring objective questions. In the first place, many teachers give partial credit (up to, perhaps, 25 percent) based on the way the question is answered. Is the answer well-organized or not? Is the English good? Is it neatly written? Others consider only relevance to the question, completeness of the answer and accuracy of the facts. However, even those who do not specifically take English and organization into account are influenced by the way an answer is written, because the clarity, accuracy, completeness and specificity of a response depend upon the way it is written. It is a good idea to ask your teacher about the things he or she thinks are important enough to a good answer to be considered in the scoring.

Another factor which may affect the way a teacher scores essay questions is the arithmetic weighting. Some teachers score essay answers by assigning intuitively an A, B, C, D or F grade. Then they give a numerical score based on the weight of the question. For example, if a question is 10 percent of an examination, the teacher might weight his letter evaluations as 10 percent of the value of that letter for a total examination, as follows:

Intuitive Letter Grade	Numerical Score
A+	10.0
A	9.5
A−	9.0
B	8.5
B−	8.0
C	7.5
C−	7.0
D	6.5
D−	6.0
F	5.5 or less

Given the scoring system illustrated above, you would feel that it pays to try to answer an essay question even if you do not know the answer because, unless the answer is too absurd, you should get partial credit.

However, not all teachers think that way. Some intuitively assign a letter grade and weight it for a 10-point question as follows:

Intuitive Letter Grade	Numerical Score
A	10.0
B	7.5
C	5.0
D	2.5
F	0.0

Or a teacher may write a model answer to each essay question and take off points based on the extent to which an answer is different from the model. Clearly, scoring of essay test questions is very subjective, which is why they are often called subjective questions. Obviously, it is important before taking an examination to get as much information as possible about the scoring techniques which will be used.

Grading of the scores. Some teachers will give you a test grade representing the "absolute" value of the sum of your answer scores. For example, if you got a summary score of 85, your grade would be B, if 72, your grade would be C−, and so on. Others prefer to "grade on the curve." Technically, this involves setting the scores into a normal probability curve. Roughly, that means setting the C range to cover the middle half of the class, the B range the next higher 20 percent, the D range the 20 percent below the C range, the A range at the top 5 percent, and the F range, the bottom 5 percent. On an examination graded this way, 5 percent are certain to get A's and 5 percent are certain to fail. Properly speaking, such a system should be used only with a fairly large class and one which approximates a normal distribution. It does not work well with a class which naturally divides into two groups, one which is pretty good and one which is pretty poor. One difficulty with grading on the curve is that it is usually assumed that the average grade will be C, but, in the nation as a whole, the average college course grade is now B.[2]

You can see that it is important, when preparing for an examination, to ask your teacher how he or she is going to score the questions and assign the grades. Your own estimation of how you rated in the course—average, below average, better than average—should reflect the actual grading system. Furthermore, your future decision about whether to take another course with this teacher may depend upon how he or she grades.

Timing of the Examination

Some teachers write exams so that time is a factor in the ultimate score. They assume that only a certain percentage of the students can finish the exam. Other teachers will either allow enough extra time for everyone to finish, or, if time is not flexible, try to write the exam so that everyone can finish it.

Content of the Examination

In addition to type of examination and scoring procedures, you should learn as much as possible about the content of the exam. (This does not include a prior look at the questions, of

---

[2] At one time, the average grade was C; the present value of B represents what colleges call grade escalation.

course, unless the exam is of the take-home variety.) Your teacher will almost certainly be willing to tell you what reading assignments and class work the test will cover. If the exam is a final, your instructor will tell you whether it covers the entire course or only those assignments and lectures since the last test.

In addition, you should ask whether any special skills will be emphasized. Some teachers of content courses also test specific skills such as reading tables or graphs. If such skills have been worked on in class, it is wise to ask if they will be covered on the examination.

Some instructors will give a review. This will cover the major points in the course as the teacher sees it. Don't miss the review class if you can possibly help it. Anyone who cuts a review class deserves to fail the exam.

Sometimes it is possible to get old examinations and study them. If the examination is printed and given annually to a large number of students, extra copies may even be sold in the college book store. In this case, it will pay you to get as many old examinations as possible and to study them carefully, answering all the questions. If old exams are not sold (and that is rare), it may be possible to get copies of exams from students who have taken the course in previous years. Duplicate a copy and study it. A word of caution, however; unless the examination is department-wide, it will not be of much use to you unless it was written by the same teacher as the one with whom you are taking the course. Different teachers of the same course often give strikingly different exams.

REVIEWING FOR OBJECTIVE EXAMINATIONS

The emphasis in objective examinations is on knowledge of facts. You may also be questioned on the opinions given by the author of your text or by your teacher. The usual viewpoint taken by a college or a university is that you need not agree with your teachers but you are expected to be familiar with their opinions respecting the materials of their courses.

In reviewing for an objective examination, it is essential to be conversant with as many of the important facts as possible. Paying special attention to those which are closely related to concepts emphasized in class will give the best chance of knowing what is to be asked in the specific questions. For example, in a course on the American Constitution, the Fourteenth Amendment will have been discussed at some length. Those Supreme Court decisions which have been important to the development of the interpretation of this amendment should be memorized. It will be useful, while reviewing, to write the most important facts, cases, examples, formulas or whatever on 3 x 5 cards and to study them over and over.

You may benefit by getting together with one or more other students from the course for which you are reviewing. Discuss which details will probably be considered important by the teacher. Then you can quiz each other until you all have some reasonable assurance that you know the details of the course well. If the test is going to be graded on the curve, you may be reluctant to do this. You may not want to help anyone else to get a better grade than you do. However, the pay-off from group work probably overrides the disadvantage of aiding your competitor under these circumstances.

REVIEWING FOR ESSAY
EXAMINATIONS

Review for essay examinations requires a different approach. Familiarize yourself with the major concepts and the special vocabulary of the discipline. Vocabulary words are often the subject of short essay questions. Respecting controversial concepts, be prepared to argue either for or against. Some essay questions consist of a statement with which you are to agree or disagree.

It is often helpful to try to guess what the essay questions will be and to mentally "write" the answers. If you have difficulty writing essay tests, it will pay for you to actually write out some answers to your imaginary questions. Try writing at first with the book open, then with the book closed. After a bit of practice, set a time limit for your answers and try to write within that limit.[3] Get another student to criticize your answers in terms of organization, clarity and so on. This is not entirely a favor; the person who helps you helps himself, too. One of the best ways to learn is to help others to learn. It may be worthwhile to exchange tutoring with students who are good at what you are not and vice versa. If you have real difficulty with any of the concepts developed in the course, formulate questions and ask the teacher for the answers.

GETTING SOME REST
BEFORE THE EXAMINATION

One thing is important. Do not cram the night before the examination, whatever kind it may be. Let your mind rest from the subject matter of the course for several hours—preferably a whole day—before you go into the exam. Relax the evening before an exam and arrange to get plenty of sleep. Go to bed early. Do not, however, take any drugs. Drugs to help you sleep will leave you dopey in the morning; it is better to lie awake than to dope yourself. Drugs designed to keep you awake so that you can study will wear off and let you down just before the exam.

Finally, don't worry. Panic on the eve of an exam can do you no good.

---

[3] Before writing answers to your questions, read the next chapter.

CHAPTER IX

Taking Examinations

Almost every undergraduate course has one or more examinations. If you have been studying throughout the semester, and if you have reviewed the material of the course, you have nothing to worry about. A few suggestions will be helpful nonetheless.

Be on time. And bring your watch. Most teachers will put the time on the blackboard at intervals during the examinations, but a watch will help you to time your answers.

Before you answer any questions, read the test instructions. Many students don't bother, and failure to read the instructions may be costly in points. Then, look over the entire examination. Are all the pages included, and are they all readable? Make a mental estimate of how long the exam will take. Will you be slow at any part? If so, try to allow a little extra time for that part.

Do the easy questions first. While you are doing them, your brain will be working on the material learned in the course. There is a good chance that, by the time you get to the harder questions, they will no longer seem hard.

Above all, get involved and ignore other students. The fact that some of them may leave the exam ahead of you does not mean that they know more; they may know less. There is no relationship between when a student leaves an examination and how much he or she knows.

ANSWERING OBJECTIVE QUESTIONS

Careful reading is the key to doing well with objective questions. If you do not read carefully, you can miss even those questions to which you know the answers. Therefore, read the instructions for each section carefully and read each question all the way through. Make sure that you know what skill is required to answer a question. For example, the following question clearly calls for an answer based on the recall of information:

The Fourteenth Amendment to the Constitution restricts the actions of:
A. The federal government, state governments, and private individuals
B. The federal government only
C. State governments only
D. Private individuals only

If you are familiar with the Fourteenth Amendment and its interpretation by the Supreme Court, you will know that the answer is C, state governments only.

In the following set of questions, the skill of making inferences based upon information contained in a graph is necessary to giving the correct answers.

Questions 10 to 13 (inclusive) require you to decide whether the statement is a valid inference from the graph. Using *only the information given in the graph,* answer:
A. if the statement can validly be inferred to be *true;*
B. if the statement can validly be inferred to be *false;*
C. if the statement *cannot validly be inferred to be either true or false.*

Percentage of eligible voters
voting in the election

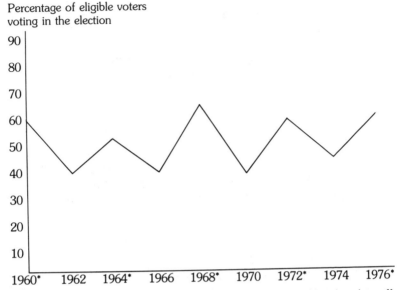

Comparison of percentage of eligible voters voting in presidential and in off-year elections, 1960–1976.

* Signifies a presidential election year.

10 _____Voter turnout for congressional and local elections is lower when no presidential candidates are running.

11 _____Republicans are less likely to go to the polls than Democrats.

12 _____The electorate is less interested in presidential than in local and congressional elections.

13 _____Richard Nixon lost the election of 1968.

Answers are 10, A; 11, C; 12, B; 13, C. Although the questions are very easy, one might have answered question 13 B if he had not read the directions carefully. Since everyone knows that Richard Nixon won the election of 1968, the temptation might be to answer this question B, false. However, the instructions call for answering the questions on the basis of information given in the graph. There is nothing in the graph to indicate who won the election; therefore; the correct answer is C.

Be sure to read all the possible answers to a question. This may prevent you from hopping onto an answer which, read quickly, seems right but isn't. For example:

> Which of the following statements concerning their terms of office is TRUE of political officeholders in the United States?
> A. The President and members of Congress serve for a term of four years.
> B. The President, members of the House of Representatives, and members of the Senate have terms of varying lengths.
> C. The President's term of office can be no more than ten years.
> D. Members of the House and Senate may not serve in office for more than two years.

The person reading this question and set of answers too quickly can easily make one of several mistakes. First, he may miss the second part of the subject in answer A and mark A true. The President does serve for a term of four years, but members of Congress do not; therefore, A is not the right answer, because an answer which is partly true and partly false, is false. Similarly, C might be marked as correct because the Twenty-second Amendment to the Constitution does limit a President to no more than ten years in office, but that is not his term of office; his term of office is 4 years. Therefore, C is wrong. Again, one might carelessly read D as correct since members of the House of Representatives have a two-year term of office. However, Senators have a six-year term. Besides, the answer does not speak of term, it speaks of service in office. There is no limit on service in office for either members of the House of Representatives or members of the Senate; they may serve as long as they can be reelected. The only possible correct answer is B.

One type of question which is often answered incorrectly because the student does not read all the answers is one in which the D answer is "All of the above." For example:

> Which of the following statements is the *best answer* concerning the terms of office of political officeholders in the United States?
>
> A. The President serves for a term of four years and may not be elected as President more than twice.
> B. Members of the House of Representatives serve a term of two years and may be reelected as often as the voters will return them to office.
> C. Senators serve a term of six years and may be indefinitely reelected.
> D. All of the above are true.

The student who is hurrying through the exam may read A, and knowing that it is true, write A as the answer to the question. If, however, he carefully reads all the answers, he will see that A, B and C are all true so that D is the best answer to the question.

Watch out for changes in the patterns of the questions. For example, among the multiple-choice questions which have four possible answers labeled A, B, C, and D, might appear the following question:

> The Revolutionary War was fought to:
>
> I. Prevent taxation without representation
> II. Eliminate the Proclamation Line barrier to western settlement
> III. Prevent encroachment on freedom of the press
> IV. Free the slaves
>
> A. I, II, III and IV
> B. I, III and IV
> C. IV only
> D. I, II and III

The answer is D. The Revolutionary War was fought for all those reasons given in I, II and III but not to free the slaves. A careless student may not even see that I, II, III and IV are not the possible answers. He may recognize I as a reason for the Revolution and put that number in the answer space without even thinking that the Roman numerals do not fit the pattern of alternative answers elsewhere in this section of the test. He will not bother to let his eye run down the page far enough to see that the possible answers are below the alternatives given in I, II, III and IV. Thus, he makes a careless mistake.

How do you deal with the harder questions? When you are not quite sure of the answer to a question, it pays to make an intelligent guess. An intelligent guess is one where you can improve the odds in your favor. Suppose a question has four answers of which you know that two are wrong. This gives you a 50-50 chance of getting the right answer. Even if your teacher is going to subtract 25 percent more for a wrong answer than for an omitted answer, it will still pay you to make a guess if you can reduce the uncertainty to only two answers. For example:

Which of the following is TRUE of the powers of the President?
A. The President is Commander-in-Chief of the armed forces.
B. The President's veto cannot be overridden by Congress under any circumstances.
C. The President appoints members of the Cabinet without the advice and consent of the Senate.
D. All of the above.

You read all the possible answers, and you know that B is incorrect; therefore, D must be incorrect, too. You have increased the odds in your favor because the answer is either A or C. It will pay you to guess; if you guess A, you are correct. A word of caution: Where you are making an intelligent guess, do not later change your answer, unless you reread the question and find that you misread it the first time. Experience shows that when a person is guessing, his first guess is more likely to be right than a later guess.

Does it pay to guess when you don't have an inkling of the right answer? It depends on how your teacher is going to score the questions. If your teacher is planning to score the questions in a way to correct for lucky guesses, it will not pay to guess when you have no information whatsoever (that is, can't eliminate some of the possibilities). However, if your teacher is going to take off the same amount for an answer omitted as for a wrong answer, it pays to guess even if you have no information. However, your chance of gaining by guessing is greatest when you always use the same letter to answer those questions which are pure guesses. Most people suggest that you always use C for your guesses since experience shows that teachers are more likely to use C as the right answer than any other letter.

Doing well on an objective test (or part of a test) depends on a good knowledge of facts and concepts given in the course and on careful reading. If, by chance, you should not understand a word in the test, ask the teacher. He or she may not tell you the meaning, but you have nothing to lose. When you finish an objective test or test section, read it over to make sure that you have not misread any of the questions or possible answers.

ANSWERING ESSAY QUESTIONS

Essay questions draw on skills different from objective questions. To do well on essay questions one must be able to organize one's information and write it down clearly and tersely.

Before starting on the essay questions, it is wise to read them all over, choose the best questions to answer, and make a preliminary estimate of how much time to spend on each answer. Unlike objective examinations, essay exams usually give the student a choice of questions. A sample direction might be:

Discuss briefly (100 to 150 words) *four* of the following:

The teacher would then give five topics from which the student is expected to answer the four he knows best. Do not answer more than the number called for unless the teacher has assured you that you will get extra credit for extra answers; otherwise, you are merely wasting your own time. Leave plenty of space between essay answers; this will make possible insertion of material which you may think of after you have finished writing a question.

Time is very precious in an essay exam, and the more you know the more precious it is. Therefore, you should estimate carefully how much time you can afford to spend on each question. The weight of the question should give you a clue. If a test is to take two hours (120 minutes), and a question is worth 10 points out of a possible 100, you should take about 12 minutes to answer it. Many students write a long answer to a 10-point question because they know a lot about it, and are then forced to cut short a 20-point question for lack of sufficient time to finish. Check your watch from time to time to make sure you are progressing with your test answers as rapidly as is consistent with finishing the test before time runs out.

Short Essay Answers

Short essay answers are those written for 5, 10, 15 or 20-point questions. They do not call for an introduction or a conclusion, merely for a clear statement of relevant and correct concepts or facts. Five-point questions not infrequently require a definition, explanation of a minor concept, or identification of a person who played a minor role. A 5-point question should require an answer not longer than 50 to 75 words if you present your information clearly. For example:

Define *electoral college.*   5 points.
The electoral college is composed of men and women chosen by the people of the states to select the President and Vice President of the United States. Each state has a number of electors equal to the number of its representatives in the Senate and the House of Representatives. The votes for President and Vice President are taken separately, and a majority of votes is needed to win.

Although there is much more that can be said about the electoral college, the answer given above should be sufficient for full credit on a 5-point question. It consists of 68 words. It is usually possible to organize such an answer in your head and get it down on paper quickly.

The 10- or 15-point question requires more development. Usually it is desirable to write a short outline of words or phrases which will recall to your mind what it is you want to say, numbered in the order in which you plan to write. For example, suppose you have the following question:

Discuss briefly the election of 1800.   15 points.

Thinking about this question you remember that in 1800 Thomas Jefferson and Aaron Burr were presidential and vice-presidential candidates on the Republican ticket. So you begin your outline, "J. Pres., B. V-P. cand. Rep. ticket." You remember, too, that Burr was favored by some of the Federalists in the House of Representatives when the election went to that house. So you note, "B. favored by Feds. for Pres. in H of R." Then you recall that the Federalist leader, Alexander Hamilton, had disliked both Jefferson and Burr; so you write down, "B. and J. disliked by Ham." Searching about in your mind for the way in which Burr came to be the Federalists' candidate for the Presidency, you suddenly recall that Burr and Jefferson tied because the Constitution did not at that time provide for separate votes in the Electoral College for President and Vice President. You note: "J. and B. tied for Pres." and "Const. not provide sep. elec. for P., V-P."

For the moment you can remember nothing additional so you number your points in the order in which you are going to write about them. As you begin to write, you recall that Jefferson had proposed to Burr that he would withhold one of the Southern Republican electors' votes from Burr so as to prevent a tie between them but that Burr had proposed instead that he (Burr) should withhold a Northern electoral vote but had not done so. You note on your outline: "J. told B. that he would withhold one

South. elec. vote from B., but B. sugg. it be a North. vote; B. did not arr. withholding." You number these to fit into your outline and continue to write. You remember that the party system had resulted in electors pledged to vote for the party's candidates so you note: "Party elec. pledged." Next you remember that the House of Representatives had a Federalist majority so you write in your outline, "Fed. maj. H. of R." Finally, you remember that during Jefferson's administration the Twelfth Amendment to the Constitution was written to change the voting provisions in the Electoral College. You add to your outline, "12th amend." Now your outline looks as follows:

2. J. Pres., B. V-P cand. Rep. ticket.
4. B. favored by Feds for Pres. in H of R.
5. B. and J. disliked by Ham.
3. J. and B. tied for Pres.
1. Const. not provide sep. elec. for P., V-P.
2b. J. told B. that he would withhold one South. elec. vote from B., but B. sugg. it be a North. vote; B. did not arr. withholding.
2a. Party elec. pledged.
3a. Fed. maj. H. of R.
6. 12th amend.

The first five points in your outline, which you wrote down before you started your answer, are numbered in the order in which you planned to include them. The last four points were thought of after you had started writing your answer, so you put the a and b after the number 2 and the a after the number 3 to indicate that these ideas would fit into your answer in that order. Following is the answer as written:

The original Constitution did not provide for separate votes for President and Vice President in the Electoral College. By 1800, the party system was already developing, and Jefferson ran for President on the Republican ticket, with Aaron Burr as his vice-presidential candidate. Each party provided for its electors to be pledged to vote for the party's candidates. When Jefferson and Burr won enough states to win a majority in the Electoral College, Jefferson told Burr that he would withhold a Southern electoral vote to avoid a tie between them. Burr said he would arrange for the withholding of a Northern electoral vote, but Burr did not do so. The resulting tie had to be settled in the House of Representatives which had a Federalist majority. Some Federalists, disliking Jefferson, supported Burr for President, but Hamilton, who, although he disliked Jefferson, hated Burr, influenced them to support the former. So Jefferson won the election. During his administration, the Twelfth Amendment to the Constitution was written to provide for separate votes for President and Vice President in the Electoral College.

By making the little outline partly before you start and partly while you are writing, you do not forget any point you have thought of, and you insure through the numbering system that you present the ideas in well-organized fashion. The answer above presents the major facts concerning the election of 1800 in only 180 words.

Note that in the two essays given above, there are no unnecessary words; the essays are, in fact, terse. Writing terse answers is important when taking an essay examination in order to cover the material called for in the time available.

What kinds of words are unnecessary? First, adjectives or clauses which add nothing to the explanation are unnecessary. Suppose, in answering the second question, you had started out: "The original Constitution, great document though it was, did not provide for separate votes for President and Vice President. . . ." "Great document though it was" is completely unnecessary; it adds nothing to the answer. It takes valuable time to write those extra five words; furthermore, your teacher has to read them, and that is likely to be annoying. Second, anything irrelevant to the answer is unnecessary. Suppose you had said at the end of the answer to the question about the election of 1800, "Burr later killed Hamilton in a duel." The duel is irrelevant; it did not occur until some years later. Including it here is mere padding. It wastes time and may even be counted against you. Adding irrelevancies is a common trick of the student who does not have very much actual information about the subject of the question and who thinks that by adding irrelevant facts he will pick up extra points. The opposite is the case. So do not pad your answers.

What about fudging? Fudging is giving a less specific rather than a more specific statement in an answer because you are not quite sure of the accuracy of the specific information. For example, imagine you are discussing the Fifteenth Amendment to the Constitution. You cannot remember the exact date of its ratification, but you remember that it came some time not long after the Civil War, along with the Thirteenth and Fourteenth Amendments. So you write: "The Fifteenth Amendment, last of the post–Civil War amendments to the Constitution. . . ." This is longer and less specific than "The Fifteenth Amendment, ratified March 30, 1870. . . ," but it's adequate. If your fudging shows understanding, your teacher will accept it. If it's incorrect or meaningless padding, it will count against you. So fudge if you must, but fudge intelligently.

Try not to repeat yourself from one question to another. To do so shows lack of depth in your understanding of one of the two questions. Even if a statement of fact is applicable to more than one answer, it usually does not count for you the second time you use it.

Long Essay Answers

The long essay, worth from 25 to 100 points, is a real test of writing skill. Since it is essentially an essay based on your memory of the content of a course rather than upon research, it must be approached in the same way as you would organize an essay paper but with the added problem of finishing in a limited time.

Despite the time limitation, it will pay you to take a few minutes to think through what you plan to say and a few more to make a formal outline to guide you while you are writing. This will help to insure that your essay is well organized.

Some essay examinations offer the student several subjects from which he or she is to choose one. Read through the possible topics and pick the one about which you have a good deal of information. Topics may tend to be general rather than specific; usually the greater number of points for the essay, the greater the degree of generality. In this case, it will be necessary to think of a particular aspect of your topic which you will develop to the exclusion of other aspects. Do not try to say everything you know about a very broad essay topic. There will not be enough time.

In doing your outline, remember that every essay has three major parts: Introduction, Body and Conclusion. Your introduction must state your topic and the aspect of it which you plan to discuss. If you are taking one side of a pro and con argument, you must make clear which side of the argument you are supporting. If any definitions are necessary, they should be in your introduction, along with any assumptions which are necessary to your argument. In other words, your introduction should say precisely what you are going to write about and give all the information necessary for an understanding of what follows.

The body of your paper must present the evidence for your argument or point of view. Evidence must be presented fairly. If there is evidence contrary to your view, it must also be noted.

Finally, the last section of your essay must offer a conclusion concerning the meaning of that information.

Major points in your outline will be those discussed above. Subpoints will be classifications of the information relevant to the aspect of the topic which you have undertaken to develop. When writing your outline, be sure to leave ample space after each section so that you can later fill in points which may occur to you as you write.

Suppose you select from the available topics the subject, "Psychological Factors Associated with Party Affiliation," on which you are to write an essay worth 50 points. Since a 50-point essay in a two-hour test would require 500 to 750 words, you should plan on an aspect of the topic broad enough to be treated completely in about that many words. Following is an example:

I. Introduction: In the United States party affiliation is essentially a psychological phenomenon.
   A. In its causes: People call themselves Democrats or Republicans because they have a feeling of attachment to their party.
   B. In its effects, psychological attachment:
      1. Causes party identification to act as a perceptual screen.
      2. Causes party affiliators to be political participants.
   C. Hypothesis: Party affiliation is essential to participation, and a decline in party affiliation is bound to lead to a decline in democratic participation.
II. Evidence
   A. In the U.S., there is little impetus to identification with party except a feeling of attachment.
      1. Generally, American parties have not had a strong ideological orientation which has drawn people in on those grounds.
      2. Our political and educational institutions do not encourage party membership.
   B. Party affiliation has important effects on affiliators.
      1. Party affiliation (identification) produces a perceptual screen so that one sees the candidates and platform of one's own party as desirable, those of the other party as undesirable.
      2. Party affiliation draws people into political participation.
         a. A sense of duty to the party draws people to participate in the campaign and to the polls.
         b. A desire to see one's party win draws even the less-politically involved to the polls.

    C. As party affiliation has declined, so has participa-
tion.
  III. Conclusion: No final conclusion can be based on the evidence.
    A. The relationship between decline in party affiliation and
the decline in voting might indicate that the first caused
the second.
    B. It might indicate that both are caused by a lack of confi-
dence in government.
    C. It might indicate that people are so satisfied with govern-
ment that they feel no need either to join a party or
go to the polls.
    D. It might indicate the converse to A.

The outline given above would, clearly, be for a fairly long essay, one which would take between a half hour and an hour to write. If less time were available, you would want to take a narrower topic.

Following is an essay based on the outline above:

PSYCHOLOGICAL FACTORS ASSOCIATED WITH PARTY AFFILIATION

In the United States party affiliation is essentially a psychological phenomenon, both in cause and in effects. People identify themselves as Democrats or Republicans because they have a feeling of attachment to the party of that name. In turn, parties have psychological effects on the people who identify with them. It is the hypothesis of this essay that party identification is an important factor in democratic citizenship, and, if it declines, democracy may also decline owing to lack of participation.

In this country, there is little to impel people to belong to a political party except a feeling of psychological identification. American parties are not strongly oriented ideologically, and there is a good deal of overlap between the issue stands of the major parties. So people do not join political parties primarily because they have a rational motivation to advance the particular ideology to which they subscribe by adhering to a party which promotes it. Further-more, there is little outside impetus to join a party. The system of representation was not planned with a view to encouraging party affiliation, and the system of education has, at least in the 20th century, tended to denigrate party attachment.

Nevertheless, during most of our history, party affiliation has been an important aspect of our political system and has had impor-tant effects on the political behavior of those who identified them-selves with a party. On the one hand, identification with a party has tended to structure the political thinking of the identifier because party identification has acted as a perceptual screen to block out favorable feelings about opposition candidates and issues and to encourage favorable feelings about the candidates and issue stands of one's own party. On the other hand, the feeling of attachment to party has tended to encourage participation in the political sys-tem. A sense of duty to party encourages some people to participate in the campaign and a great many more to go to the polls. In addition, the impulse to register and vote even among the relatively apolitical is enhanced by the desire to see one's party win the election—entirely apart from what one may get out of the election personally.

The importance of the relationship between party affiliation and political participation is manifested by the fact that in recent history, as more and more people have dropped out of political parties and become "independent," the participation in elections has also tended to drop. Indeed, the participation of eligible voters in the 1976 election was perilously close to 50 percent.

It might be concluded that the correlation between a low level of party affiliation and the low level of voting participation demon-strates that lack of party affiliation impedes the democratic process since there is a lack of motivation for voters to participate. On the other hand, the relationship may indicate merely that people have lost confidence in government and thus neither join parties nor go to the polls. Conversely, it is possible that low affiliation and low participation simply mean that people are satisfied with government and feel no need to join parties and participate in government. Finally, it might mean that, when a person does not go to the polls, there is no reinforcement for attachment to party so that the decline in participation is the cause of the decline in party affiliation, rather than the other way around. No final conclusion can be drawn about the meaning of the relationship.

The above essay is about 575 words.

REREADING THE FINISHED EXAMINATION

Whether your examination was all objective, all essay or a combination of the two, it will pay you to reread it when you are finished. It is easy, when working fast, to make errors, to misread questions and possible answers, to omit a word and thus turn a correct into an incorrect statement, or to make a silly statement. Try to allow time to read your exam over carefully, to correct errors in spelling and punctuation, to eliminate silly statements, and to insert necessary additional information. Even if you have only a few minutes, at least skim what you have written to pick up serious bloopers; you may save yourself several points on your grade.

REVIEWING THE GRADED EXAMINATION

When your graded examination is returned to you, it is wise to review it, preferably with the teacher. The purpose of such a review is not to persuade the teacher to change the grade—though sometimes a student can get an improved grade—but to find out why the exam got the grade it did. If you find that your grade is lower than you had hoped because you did not understand the material of the course, you need to review your general study patterns. If your problem was failure to read the questions correctly, make a mental effort to read more carefully the next time you take an examination.

However, if you knew the material well but failed to communicate your ideas in your essays, you need to practice writing examination answers. Before your next essay exam, practice writing answers to questions which you think might turn up on the examination. Time yourself and try to learn to organize and present your ideas more effectively. With practice, your exam grades will show improvement.

CHAPTER X

After College, Where?

After you get your college degree, what are you going to do? Will you get a job and start your life career or will you stay on in school?

Most people in our society drift into their life work. They need money; they look for a job; they stick with it until fired or laid off or until, it is to be hoped, a better opportunity comes along. For a few people, the future is absolutely cut and dried; they get the necessary education to fill a place in a relative's business or professional office. They have an assured future, but they never have the adventure of wondering what the next step will be, living in unexpected places, doing unexpected things. The optimum is probably somewhere in between. Find out what you want to do; get the education you need to do it; look for a good opportunity to do what you want, and, when it comes along, seize it.

It is beyond the scope of this book to give you detailed information on your post-graduate career. However, it will raise some questions and give some suggestions for finding information which will help you plan your career.

MORE SCHOOL OR A JOB

It is possible to have a perfectly satisfactory and lucrative career without going to graduate or professional school. On the other hand, some careers are impossible without professional education, and some are more likely to be successful if you have additional education. So ask yourself a few questions before you make a decision. And start asking them no later than your sophomore year in college; don't wait until graduation is two months away.

How are you going to feel about more education after four years of college? Are you going to be tired of school and the dependency on others which usually accompanies student status? If so, get a job after graduation. If you later find that you want more education, you can come back; one of the nice things about the American school system is that it is open to people of almost any age.

Maybe you are planning to go on in school because you are afraid to face the outside world. Some people never want to leave the familiar routine of classes and study. Be honest with yourself. If you are staying in school because you are frightened of "the real world," you should get out and get a job; you need the experience of independence for your own self-development.

However, if you love study and have career aims that demand additional education, stay in school and get it right away if you can afford it. Now is the time because your study skills should be honed to their sharpest by the time you graduate from college.

Do your ultimate career aims require more education? If you are going into medicine, law, college teaching, scientific research or any one of a number of other fields, get at least some of your professional education immediately. Without one to four additional years of training, you will find no job openings in your field. In some fields, additional training may not be absolutely necessary but will be desirable. For example, suppose you have taken a degree in chemistry, but you want to go into the business management end of the chemical industry. A master's degree in business administration would be very helpful in getting a job which would lead where you want to go. In some fields, work experience before getting any additional education may be not only possible but desirable. Furthermore, some companies pay for advanced education for promising young executives; you may be able to save yourself the cost of further education by getting it at the expense of your company. Ask the librarians at your school where you can find more information about the various options respecting job opportunities and educational requirements. Talk to the college placement service. Then make your decision about further education. Finally, if you are not absolutely certain what you want to do in life, a few years experience on the job may help to clarify your objectives.

Do your college records indicate you could benefit from more education? Although this book is designed to help you get the highest possible grades, it would be unrealistic to expect everyone to get A's and B's. There is much more to college than just the academic work. Some C-average students go out and make a tremendous career in business or some other field. If you are just a so-so student, but you have talents in dealing with people or in another area which does not show up in your grade-point average, go out and get a job where you can utilize the talents you have. If you haven't taken advantage of the resources of your college's career counseling service (or whatever it is called), do so now. You may find that your talent at winning college elections or just making friends can be translated into a satisfying career. However, if your grades are really excellent, and you enjoy study and research, try to plan to continue your education.

Can you afford more education now? Some students would like to go on, but they contemplate the weight of loans or the toll that their education costs are taking of their family's income, and they reluctantly go out to look for work. Before you do that, if you really want further education, see if you can't find a scholarship or, preferably, a fellowship (which offers some money for living expenses as well as tuition). The college career counseling service may be able to help you. The chairperson of your major department might be a good source to consult. Again, the librarians at your college can direct you to literature which will tell you where to find financial aid in various educational fields. Finally, the schools to which you apply will know about financial aid available through their admissions offices.

GETTING INTO GRADUATE OR PROFESSIONAL SCHOOL

Criteria for Admission

Graduate and professional schools base their admissions primarily on three criteria: Academic accomplishment, scholastic aptitude and personal qualities.[1] Many schools also take minority status into consideration.[2]

Academic accomplishment. Academic accomplishment is determined mostly by your grades. If you happen to be graduating from a college which is outstanding either for its exceptionally high quality or for its exceptionally poor quality, that will be taken into consideration in evaluating the meaning of your grade point average. It is not always necessary to have an A or B average, but it helps. In some fields, it will be virtually impossible to get into school with less. Sometimes routinely and sometimes to help in the evaluation of your academic accomplishments, a graduate

---

[1] Although few of them will admit it openly, professional schools and possibly also graduate departments sometimes admit less-qualified people who can, or whose parents can, make sizeable contributions to the school's endowment ahead of better-qualified but financially less well-off applicants. If you fall into the category of the financially well-endowed, you may be able to get in by this route. However, the school which admits you does not guarantee to graduate you, and the academic going may be very stiff.

[2] In Regents of the University of California v. Allan Bakke (1977), the United States Supreme Court held specific minority quotas to be a violation of equal protection of the laws but did not rule out the possibility of giving consideration to minority status in granting admission.

school may ask you to submit a paper done during your college years. Requirement of the submission of a paper is fairly common among law schools. (If you have no very good paper, you may be tempted to submit someone else's which you think is better. Don't! Such dishonesty, if discovered, could cost you admission to the profession of your choice.)

Scholastic aptitude. To measure scholastic aptitude, a number of graduate and professional schools now require applicants to take a standardized aptitude test oriented to the skills needed in their field. Examples of these are the Graduate Record Examination and the Law School Admissions Test. If you are required to submit a test score, plan to take the test at the end of your junior year or beginning of your senior year in college. The July or October (approximately) exam dates are best for those planning to enter professional school the following fall. They allow you time for another exam to be taken and submitted for school consideration in case your first exam score is unexpectedly low,[3] but they are close enough to the admission date to be acceptable to the professional school admissions offices. If you plan to enter school in the spring, take your test initially in December or February.

The Educational Testing Service which administers most of these tests maintains that you cannot study for them specifically, that your native abilities and your general educational background are all that is measured. However, an extensive and lucrative business in training for the advanced education tests has grown up in recent years. Whether these courses really improve the scores of a significant number of candidates, I don't know. Students are convinced that they do. To the extent that having taken a course will allay your panic and make it easier for you to do well, it probably pays to take one if you can afford it. The courses do offer practice in taking tests under simulated test conditions,

---

[3] You will receive your test scores about a month after taking the test.

and they give an opportunity to become familiar with the directions for the various segments of the test, some rules of thumb for taking tests and some review of the academic skills tested. However, if you are self-disciplined and honest with yourself, you can probably do the same thing by buying one or more of the study books on the market and studying them on your own time. Also, the Educational Testing Service will send you a sample exam. Study that, at least.

To apply for one of the admissions tests administered by the ETS, write to the Educational Testing Service, Princeton, New Jersey 08540 or pick up an application at the admissions office of a nearby professional or graduate school in the field of your interest. If the school you have in mind administers its own tests or uses tests from another testing service (which is unlikely), the admissions office can tell you. In order to find out the requirements of admission to the professional schools in your field, call up or write to the admissions offices of several of them.

If the test you take is administered by the ETS, it will be given at a testing center somewhere near your present school. To insure that you are able to take the exam you want, apply and pay your fee in advance; this will guarantee you a place at the examination. It is possible to take these exams on a walk-in basis, paying the fee at the time, but there is no guarantee that you will get in. If all the available places are taken, you will not.

The ETS offers its test takers a service which assembles their data for admission to professional schools. It collects college transcripts from all the schools a student has attended at the undergraduate level. The grades on these are summed up and translated into a grade point average based on a 4-point scale, standardized for all applicants so that each GPA can readily be compared with GPAs for all other applicants. In most cases, the GPA which is computed will be based on the first six semesters' work (since the decisions concerning admission are usually made while the applicant is completing his or her senior year in college). Usually transcripts for work completed during the senior year must be mailed directly to the professional or graduate school admission office.

Personal qualities.   Schools have three sources of information about your personal qualities: your letter of application, letters of recommendation from those who know you, and personal interviews.

When you write your application letter or fill out the application form for a school to which you are applying, study carefully the instructions and questions which come with the school's application materials. Be sure you cover every bit of information the school asks for. Organize your letter carefully, write an outline and rough draft, then let your letter cool for a couple of days. Correct the spelling, punctuation, grammar, and style. Errors in this letter can cost you your admission. Retype the entire letter neatly and send it in with all the other required materials.

Letters of recommendation are requested from your Dean or the chairperson of your major department and from professors who have had you in their classes. Letters from others who know you and your work well are also desirable. For example, a letter from a professional in the field that you plan to enter who has had the opportunity to know your work as an apprentice in that field can be very helpful in gaining you admission to the school of your choice. The application materials from the admissions offices of the schools to which you apply will tell you what kind of letters of recommendation are wanted. Where you have a choice, it is only common sense to ask for recommendation letters from people who know you well and who you know think well of you. When you ask someone for a letter of recommendation, give that person a list of your accomplishments. Do not concentrate on your academic work; the school to which you are applying already has a source of that kind of information. Stress your co-curricular activities and off-campus activities—service on the University Senate, membership in a special interest group on or off campus, tutoring of high school students, volunteer work,

constructive hobbies, relevant work experiences, church or syna-
gogue activities and the like.

Some schools require interviews of every applicant. Others
make them available to any applicant who wants to have one.
Still others make them available only when students have good
enough grades and admission test scores to make them possible
candidates for admission.

There is no formula for a good interview. The interviewer's
criteria for admission will depend upon the field of training. For
example, if the field is one dealing with people, especially sick
people or helpless people, the interviewer will be looking for
qualities of warmth and understanding. However, in another field,
such qualities might be quite irrelevant or even counter-productive.
The general rule for going to an admissions interview is common
sense. *Be on time.* Dress simply but appropriately. Leave your
blue jeans at home. If you are a female, don't wear excessively
high heels; they give an impression of frivolousness. If you are
male, be sure your hair and beard (if any) are neatly trimmed
and combed. Don't smoke unless invited to; it offends some people. Don't chew gum. Answer questions candidly, but stick to
the subject. Don't volunteer information about your political or
personal views. It probably pays to do a little advance thinking
in case you should be asked why you want to go into this field
or some similar question. If you can jot down a few points and
then memorize them, it will help you not to be tongue-tied. Otherwise, be as natural as possible.

Where to Apply

In applying to graduate or professional schools, it is wise to
apply only to those where you have a good opportunity of being
accepted. Application fees are high, and most people want to
apply to several schools; why waste your money trying to get
into a school which is certain to turn you down? You may want
to take advantage of the ETS Candidate Referral Service which

GUILDENSTERN PROFESSIONAL SCHOOL
APPLICATIONS AND ACCEPTANCES, FALL 1980

Each cell shows the relationship of applicants (figure to the left of the slash) to acceptees (figures to the right of the slash) for that combination of GPA and professional school admission test score.

| | PROFESSIONAL SCHOOL ADMISSION TEST SCORE | | | | | | | | | | | |
	Below 300	300 349	350 399	400 449	450 499	500 549	550 599	600 649	650 699	700 749	750 up	Totals
4.00 3.75			2/0		3/0	9/9	7/7	7/7	4/4	2/2		34/29
3.74 3.50			1/0	5/0	7/1	25/20	26/25	20/20	10/10	3/3		97/79
3.49 3.25		2/0	1/0	5/0	11/0	45/25	52/50	26/26	9/9	1/1		152/111
3.24 3.00	1/0	3/0	3/0	8/0	18/2	55/20	82/81	45/45	11/11	2/2	1/1	229/162
2.99 2.75	1/0	2/0	5/0	4/0	16/3	50/18	72/43	40/40	15/15	1/1	1/1	207/121
2.74 2.50	1/0	3/0	8/0	16/0	16/1	25/8	30/15	16/14	8/8	1/1		124/47
2.49 2.25	2/0	2/0		13/0	12/0	15/1	11/3	14/10			1/1	70/15
2.24 2.00	1/0		1/0	3/0	3/0	1/0	6/0	5/2	2/2			22/4
Below 2.00	1/0	1/0	2/0			1/0						5/0
Totals	7/0	13/0	23/0	54/0	86/7	225/101	287/224	173/164	59/59	10/10	3/3	940/568

UNDERGRADUATE GRADE POINT AVERAGE

is available in some fields. If you are registered for ETS Data Assembly Service, your record will be circulated to schools to which you have not even applied. If your status or your record is especially noteworthy in respect to the school's particular needs, you may be invited to apply. In order to take advantage of this option, however, you must apply to the ETS early. The option is probably most valuable to members of significant minorities or to those students whose residence would give the school a more interesting geographical balance than the run-of-the-mill applicant. In deciding where to apply, consult any of the books which give information about schools' admission standards in your chosen field. For example, the Association of American Law Schools and the Law School Admission Council together publish each year a *Prelaw Handbook* which lists all the accredited law schools in the United States and its territories; for each school a two-page statement is given which sums up the program, describes the student body, explains admission requirements, indicates costs and available financial aid and, for most schools, offers a matrix showing LSAT (Law School Admissions Test) and GPAs of students who applied and students who were admitted.

In making your applications, it is desirable, within your financial ability, to select one school where you are a little bit to the left and below the bulk of the previous year's acceptances and one where you are a little bit to the right and above them. The former, if you get in, will test your ability to the utmost; the latter is your "back-up" school. For the rest, try to hit the average of the acceptances for the previous year. Your chances of both getting in and getting an education suited to your ability are best here.

FINDING A DECENT JOB

What a decent job is depends on your objectives in getting it. If you are planning to work for only a few months or a couple of years to save up enough money to go to graduate school, the job that pays the most is probably the job you will consider decent. However, if your job is going to be the first step in your career, the pay will be only one of several considerations. What follows is concerned only with jobs of the second kind, that is, career-oriented.

Getting the job you want in the field you want is not something you begin only after graduation. Aside from getting the education you need and the grades to show you have done well in it, there is much you can do while you are still in college to help you get a good job when you get out.

Before-Graduation Jobs

If possible, get a temporary job in your chosen field during summer vacations. Quite frequently jobs are available which will give you good training and be helpful to you after you graduate by bringing you in contact with people who are already successful in the field. One student who planned to become a lawyer worked during her summer vacations as secretary to a lawyer. Others with the same objective have gotten jobs as legal assistants or as library assistants working in law libraries. Premedical students sometimes get jobs as aides or orderlies in hospitals. Unfortunately, such jobs are sometimes not as well paid as the pure muscle jobs which are also available to college students. You will have to make the choice about balancing extra money now against experience that will pay off in the future.

Another before-graduation possibility may be an apprentice program at your school. More and more schools are offering college credit for off-campus educational experience outside the classroom. Some even require it. If you can find the time in your college program, such an experience in your field will be extremely valuable. It can give you an advance taste of your chosen profession. You might learn that this field is not for you. If so, you have certainly learned something worth knowing. Most people, however, find that they do like their field, and the job they have during their off-campus education frequently gives them experience they could get in no other way, often develops valuable contacts which are useful after graduation and may even lead to a permanent job. Occasionally, too, such jobs carry pay, but usually not. Consult your advisor about the possibility of apprentice education through the college you attend.

If you do not have a job already lined up when you are expecting to graduate, and most people do not, it is wise to make a careful assessment of yourself, of available jobs, and of the future job market.

Assessing Yourself

By now you should be familiar with the resources available for assessing yourself. Review your personal file and make note of your strengths, weaknesses and objectively-determined preferences. If you have not taken a vocational preference and other job-related tests, go to the career counseling service at your college and take them.

Examine your values. What matters most to you? Do you want a very well-paid profession? What else is important to you in a job? Adventure? Security? Opportunities to do research? A chance to meet interesting people? These are not just idle questions. Psychological research shows that satisfaction in the work you do is a major factor in happiness generally.

Assessing the Job Market

Probably the first place to go if you are trying to find out what job options are open to you is your college placement office. The chances are that, early in your senior year, you will receive some kind of notice from that office indicating what its services are and inviting you to a preliminary lecture or seminar. Usually the fee charged is nominal or nothing. The placement service will have information on all kinds of jobs, part-time, temporary, summer and permanent. It will be able to help you assess the job market, and it will also serve as a liaison between you and those companies which send out recruiters to college campuses with a view to picking out some future executives. Above all, it will give you a chance to sit down with someone who knows the ropes and discuss your background and your preferences and get some advice on how to go about getting a job.

Another possibility is your friendly college library. Here you can find books on how to get a job, on job opportunities for people with various kinds of aptitudes and training, and on pay scales in the various fields. Most important, you can get recent government statistics and estimates of the probable future national need for people in various fields and subfields. These are important statistics. Most people graduating with a Bachelor's degree have a broad enough background for many options respecting their future work. At the time when you are taking your first steps into the job market, it is sensible to look ahead ten or more years to try to get some feeling for where you will be if you take one road as opposed to another.

Getting a Job

Where to look. In deciding where to look for work, be sure to consider all the possibilities. You are, after all, considering a lifetime career. Don't, through ignorance or prejudice, overlook something that might be a good opportunity. Most people think first of the field of private industry which is, of course, the major source of employment in our economic system. However, there is an enormous variety of jobs available in the government services, federal, state and local. These usually offer good pay, good fringe benefits and excellent vacation and sick leave. Opportunities for advancement will depend on the size of the governmental unit, the policy concerning promotion (within the agency only or across agency lines) and the degree to which the service is politicized (hires and promotes for political rather than managerial reasons). Jobs in the federal service have in the past been stepping-stones to excellent opportunities in private industry. Recent legislation has made moving from federal to private employment somewhat more difficult, but it seems likely that Congress will either abolish these restrictions or reduce the time periods involved. Besides, there is some question as to whether restrictions on personal rights to employment could stand up to a court test.

A third possibility is the military. This entails a rather special kind of life, and you would be wise to make sure that it is for you before committing yourself. Again, the training and the contacts in the military are sometimes stepping-stones to good jobs outside.[4]

Finally, don't overlook the possibility of going into business for yourself if you think your own interests will be best served by doing so. You will need money, however, and new small businesses do not have a highly satisfactory record of success. If you do decide to go into business for yourself, get as much relevant information as possible about the problems of managing the kind of business you intend. The documents librarian in your college library can help you to find sources of government information (of which there is a great deal), and the reference librarian can direct you to useful material from nongovernment sources. The college placement service can also help you, in all probability.

Who can help you?   As already noted, one of your sources of information about actual job openings will be the college placement service. Another possibility is the public employment services operated by the state and local authorities. These will list jobs in private industry. Other jobs in private industry will be listed with private employment agencies and in the newspapers and other publications. The placement service can give you advice on where to look for published job listings in the field of your interest.

If you are interested in one of the government services, you will probably have to take one or more civil service exams. During

---

[4] One of the sources of undergraduate scholarships is the military services. If you accept such a scholarship, you will be expected to serve as an officer for a period of four years.

your senior year, it is not at all a bad idea to take as many of these as your educational qualifications allow. This way you will get on many civil service registers. You will be ranked according to your score on the examination, with veterans getting preference. So, especially if you are a veteran, do not overlook the possibility of government service. Anyone interested in the federal civil service should call or write to the nearest United States Office of Personnel Management or Federal Job Information Center. Your telephone directory is also a good source; it will list the government agencies for your state and locality. A telephone call or two will locate for you the hiring unit or units for government agencies in your area.

Finally, the people you know may be able to help you. Ask members of your family, former employers, and teachers to keep you in mind if they should hear of a job which you might fill.

What should you do?   Prepare a resumé. Every job hunter should have a carefully prepared data sheet giving name, address and telephone number; the kind of position sought; and a summary of work experience, education and references. On page 117 is a sample resumé for an imaginary college graduate. Note that it is neatly typed, with appropriate headings for each kind of entry. Under the section on education in the model, only the basic facts have been entered, but should you have any honors—Dean's List, Cum Laude, Honors in your major, noteworthy co-curricular activity—be sure to enter them, too. Be sure to enter all part-time and full-time jobs which might have a bearing on your eligibility for the position you want.

On the other hand, do not overload your resumé with irrelevancies, even if they are something to be proud of. Such padding looks like self-puffery and produces a negative effect on the reader. Furthermore, if your resumé is not too long, it is more likely to be read by every person who has something to say about your getting the job you want. Job seekers learn to use judgment about what to include and what to leave out. As you advance, only the more important jobs should be included. For example, at

Arthur H. Jones
95 Crimson Lane
Remington, N.Y. 10449   Telephone
                                     (516) 421-9832

Employment Goal: Copywriter in an advertising agency or junior editor in a publishing house.

Education: Guildenstern University, 1975–1979
Hamworth, New York 10551
Major: English Literature
Minor: Fine Arts
B.A.: June 1979; GPA: 3.52

Remington High School, 1971–1975
Remington, New York 10449
Diploma: 1975; Class Rank: 26-101

Employment: 1977 to present (20 hrs. per week plus occasional overtime and full-time during summers.)
Computer operator   Supervisor:
Data Gatherers, Inc.   Mr. George Kent
322 Ashford Avenue   Tel.: (516) 433-4756
Hamworth, New York 10551

1976–1977 (time variable)
Operated circular delivery service, Your-Ad, Sir. This business, started with financial aid from my father, was a success, but it took too much time from school work, so I sold it. The work involved mostly circular deliveries, in connection with which I supervised two teenaged boys. A less profitable but more interesting part of the business was designing and printing, on a home printing press, circulars for 15 local businesses. Sample circulars available on request.

1975–1976 (15 hours per week.)
Lifeguard at the YMCA indoor pool
Hamworth YMCA   Supervisor:
Hamworth, New York 10551   Mr. Henry Smith
                                  Tel.: (516) 472-9774

Recommendations: (in addition to above)

Dr. Allen Harkness, Assoc. Prof. of Fine Arts
Fine Arts Department, Guildenstern University

Dr. Christian Lester, Professor of Literature
English Department, Guildenstern University

Dr. Mary Parsons
Dean of Liberal Arts, Guildenstern University

your level of college graduate, it might not be appropriate to list baby-sitting jobs which you held in high school unless such work is particularly relevant to the job for which you are applying. Baby-sitting experience might be mentioned if you were applying for a job at a nursery school but not if you were aiming to become an advertising executive. In making up your resumé, first list everything which seems relevant; then discuss the list with someone who has experience and revise it accordingly; finally, type the list in good form.

Make contacts with employers. Many of these contacts will be arranged for you through your college placement office or an employment agency, but some you may arrange yourself by simply calling up for a job which you see listed or that someone mentions to you. You may make other contacts by writing to potential employers who have advertised or who you think may have openings in which you would be interested. Be sure to send a copy of your resumé.

Go out on interviews. If an employer is interested in you, he or she will want an interview. You would not get one if the employer did not think you had some qualifications for the job.

The interview is critical. When you are asked to come in, always inquire about directions. An address is often not sufficient; many are very hard to find. If you are coming by public transportation, ask what bus or train to take and where to get off. Usually the person in the employment agency or on the other end of the telephone will tell you which way to go after you get off the train or bus, but, if he doesn't, ask. Similarly, if you are coming by car, get directions to the door. Good directions are essential to being on time, and being on time is the first step to getting the job.

Dress conservatively. For an interview for any kind of office job, a suit is recommended for either a man or a woman. Probably a woman is wise not to wear a pants suit for the first interview. Also, she should be sparing of makeup and wear sensible shoes. Boots or excessively high heels may make a bad impression. Similarly, a man should wear a tie, not a turtleneck. All hirsute adornment (hair) should be well-groomed, and nails should be clean and filed.

Demeanor is important. As suggested for admissions interviews, don't smoke unless asked to, and don't chew gum. Answer questions candidly and fully, but do not volunteer information or, unless asked, opinions. Never run down a previous employer. Don't make too much of an issue of salary. You will probably be informed of the salary range in which the job falls; if not, you can ask the range toward the end of the interview, especially if it has gone well enough for you to feel that you are being favorably considered. The interviewer will probably indicate when the interview is over by asking you if you have any further questions, and, if you don't, by standing up, shaking your hand and telling you that the company will let you know. Be sure that you leave a copy of your resumé with the interviewer if he or she does not already have one.

After the interview is over, give the company time to make a decision. Don't call back too quickly. However, if several weeks have gone by, or if you are thinking of taking another job but would rather have this one, a call is desirable. Ask for the person with whom you had the interview. Say that you are interested in learning whether the company has made a decision yet. Usually that will either get an answer or get a statement concerning when an answer can be expected.

Don't grab the first job that is offered to you unless you really think you want it and that it will lead where you want to go. It is better to get a temporary job to keep you going financially until you find the right thing than to take something you don't really want or that leads nowhere.

When you do get a job, take time to write a brief letter to those other employers who have been sufficiently interested in your qualifications to be considering you for a position. Not only is that the considerate and mannerly thing to do, but at some time in the future you might want a job with one of them. Just say, "Thank you for considering me but, after careful thought, I have decided to take a position with the X Company."

How much of what you have learned in college will you use in later life? That depends on the career you choose. Once you settle into a business or a profession, you may find that you are using little of the specific content of the knowledge you acquired in college. But the skills you have learned—to read well, to analyze material presented to you, to do research, to remember what you need to know—are certain to be of value to you, probably more than you are aware of.

APPENDIX A

Tools of the Student

A six-year-old going off to school on the first day proudly carries a new pencil box filled with pencils and an eraser. These are the minimum tools of a primary school pupil. Similarly, every college student should have a set of minimum tools. They are listed below.

DICTIONARY

A good dictionary is essential for the desk of any college student.[1] It is worth a substantial investment because it lasts a great many years. Although the language does change, the usefulness of a dictionary will outlast that of most textbooks by many years.

In buying a dictionary, use care. Just because a dictionary has the name "Webster" across the front does not guarantee its worth. The name is now in the public domain,[2] and anyone can use it. A dictionary should be published by a publishing house which

---

[1] I am grateful to my colleague, Dr. Wilbur Scott, Professor of English at New College of Hofstra University, for his help in developing criteria of a good dictionary.

[2] In the public domain means that the name is no longer covered by copyright law restricting its use to a particular person or publisher.

has editors specialized in the work of lexicography. Check the first few pages to see who were responsible for editing the dictionary and what were their qualifications. See if it has a preliminary guide to its use and whether it has, at the bottom of each double page, a summary of the symbols used to describe word derivations and pronunciations. A dictionary for college students should have 1500 or more pages devoted only to the words in the language, their meanings, usages, pronunciations and derivations.

In addition to their primary function, many dictionaries have scholarly articles at the beginning about various aspects of language and supplementary sections at the end. A good dictionary should be the source of biographical, historical and geographical information.

GRAMMAR BOOK

A good reference grammar is an essential. Spend enough to get one which is complete. Grammars used in standard college English courses may or may not be adequate from this point of view. Some of them are too brief because they review only the essentials of good English. A reference grammar should have complete rules for the English language, including the less-commonly used grammatical structures. Look for one published by a reputable publisher, in which it is easy to quickly find the particular rule of usage, grammar, punctuation, sentence structure, and the like that you may need when writing a paper. Your English teacher or the college or university librarian can help you to choose a serviceable book.

PERSONAL FILE

Everyone past high school age needs a personal file. The college student's file should contain:

Complete school records, including both high school and college transcripts.

Records and reports of any special tests that he or she has taken. Of course, this includes SAT or ACT scores.

Any papers which he or she has written. These should include a clean copy of the original as the paper was handed in to the instructor, and the original, marked up with the instructor's comments, if it was returned.

Any other material which seems to be pertinent to the student's career in school or at work.

Insurance papers, medical records, and so on.

A file box to keep them in an alphabetical classification of some kind.

COLLEGE BULLETINS

Students should keep a copy of the college bulletin or bulletins for the year in which they entered every school they have attended. The bulletin is in the nature of a contract between students and the college or university. With some exceptions,[3] so long as students meets the requirements for the degree as listed in the bulletin of their year of entrance, the degree cannot be refused. Students can elect to graduate under requirements published later in their college career but may choose to stick with the requirements in the bulletin of their entering year.[4]

In addition to graduation requirements, college bulletins include information about the school's facilities and services, financial aid, credit by examination, the names and qualifications of members of the faculty and administration and other useful information. Furthermore, the course descriptions given in college bulletins are a guide to admissions officers in assigning transfer credit to incoming transfer students.

---

[3] These have to do with students who drop out and return after a lapse of time and may vary from school to school.

[4] State laws may vary with the degree to which the bulletin is binding on the school.

TYPEWRITER

Every student ought to have a typewriter and know how to use it fairly well. Colleges usually require that papers be typed, and paying someone else to do it is expensive. You can learn to type from a book or take a course during the summer if you have not already learned how.

It is probably best to have a well-made portable typewriter. However, check the operation of any portable you buy before you invest in it. Some portable typewriters have a very slow action, and some are given to strikeovers.

APPENDIX B

Using
the College Library

Your years in college should make you familiar with the library as a tool of learning. A knowledge of how to use a library is invaluable to anyone who may ever have to do a research job of any kind. Since college libraries are much more extensive than high school libraries, the skill of library use is one advantage that the college graduate has over the high school graduate—provided that he or she has taken advantage during college years of the opportunity to learn.

PARTS OF THE COLLEGE LIBRARY

Reading Areas

Since libraries are used for reading and study, they always have reading areas. Older libraries, which usually had closed stacks,[1] had one or more rooms used only for reading. Modern

---

[1] A library which has closed stacks requires readers to fill out a "call slip" for each book to be used. This slip is taken to a circulation desk; the book is searched in the stacks, and the reader picks it up when it reaches the circulation desk. Because of the danger of losing irreplaceable materials, all libraries have closed stacks for some of their collections.

libraries, which usually have open stacks,[2] often have reading areas within the stacks themselves. Since smoking is forbidden in most areas, many libraries feature a smoking room fitted out as a reading room. Books used in most of the reading areas of an open-stacks library need not be signed out. Furthermore, books no longer needed may simply be left on the desk of the reading room; library personnel will reshelve them.

In addition to these areas, all college libraries have a reserve room and a periodical reading room, both of which will be discussed later. Small private study quarters, called carrels, are also available. These are usually assigned to particular individuals; unfortunately, carrels in many libraries are not sufficient in number for undergraduates to use them. They are mostly reserved for faculty members and graduate students who are doing long-term research projects. Most libraries also have special desks which can be reserved. The advantage of a reserved desk or carrel is that one can keep books there and not have to lug them back and forth from school to home or dorm. Books which are to be left at an assigned study or desk must be signed out at the circulation desk, at least in most libraries.

The Card File

The card file consists of a number of standing cases located in the main reading room or in an adjacent room. These cases have removable drawers which are filled with cards. Almost every book in the library will have at least three cards in the card file, one each for the author, the title, and the subject discussed in it. Since most books will be classified under more than one subject, they will usually have more than three cards. If you cannot find a card in the card file for the book you have in mind, the library does not possess it.[3]

---

[2] A library which has open stacks allows readers to find their own materials on the shelves.

[3] An exception is government documents, some of which may be catalogued only in the Documents Room.

Subdivision. The card file may be subdivided into three sections: by author, with all books listed alphabetically according to the author and, within the author category, alphabetically by titles; by titles, with all books listed alphabetically by titles; and by subject, with the contents of the library subdivided according to predetermined subject categories, then alphabetically by author and then by title. Sometimes a card file is subdivided into only two categories: author-title and subject. Sometimes it is undivided, the subjects being mixed in among the authors and the titles, all alphabetically.

Using the card file. If you know what book you are looking for, simply find it by either author or title in its appropriate alphabetic location.

If the card is an author card, it will contain the name of the author at the top, last name first, the title, the publishing information and notes as to number of pages and illustrations, bibliography, and so on, if any are present. In the upper left-hand corner will be the call number which enables you to find the book on the shelves of the stacks. Some call numbers have "Ref.," "Doc.," "Oversize," or other notations above them. "Ref." means that the book is available in the Reference Room, "Doc." that it is available in the Documents Room, "Oversize" that the book is on a special shelf in the stacks where oversized books are shelved. Some libraries use additional notations, such as "Special collections," to indicate where books are kept. Sometimes a library will have several copies of a book, one of which is in "Ref." or "Doc." If you wish to take out a book which is in one of these special places, note whether there is a second card which indicates the presence on the regular shelves of a copy additional to the reference or documents copy. "Ref.," "Doc.," and "Special Collections" books are usually not allowed to leave the library. At the bottom of each card is a list of subjects covered in the book, which you can find in the card file for other books on the same subject. If the card is a title card, the title will be listed at the top, then the author, title again and so on as for an author card.

```
CT105
 .R4      Rees, Goronwy, 1909
            The multimillionaires,
          six studies in wealth,
          New York, Macmillan,
          1961

          128p. 22 cm.

              Full name: Morgan
              Goronwy Rees

          1. Millionaires. I. Title
```

Author Card

```
CT105       The multimillionaires
 .R4      Rees, Goronwy, 1909
            The multimillionaires,
          six studies in wealth,
          New York, Macmillan,
          1961

          128p. 22cm.

              Full name: Morgan
              Goronwy Rees

          1. Millionaires. I. Title
```

Title Card

If you have only a subject in mind, look up your topic in the subject file. On a subject card, the subject will be listed at the top in capital letters. Some libraries type the subject in red ink. Some cards include additional information such as the birth and

```
CT105      Millionaires
  .R4      Rees, Goronwy, 1909
           The multimillionaires,
           six studies in wealth.
           New York, Macmillan,
           1961

           128p. 22cm.


           Full name: Morgan
           Goronwy Rees


           1. Millionaires. I. Title
```

Subject Card

death dates of the author, a summary of the book's contents and so on. If you are doing research, it is essential to note the call number, author(s), title and complete publishing information on a 3 × 5 card. Also note any special information regarding location. This becomes your bibliography card, and you make other notations on it to suit your own needs.[4]

Stacks

To find the book(s) you are looking for, go to the stacks. These are arranged in tiers (floors). The number of the tier on which the call number of your book can be found will be shown somewhere in the card file room and probably in the stack elevator as well.

Finding the book in the stacks. Books are shelved in the stacks according to the call numbers of one or the other of two main classification systems, the Dewey Decimal system or the Library of Congress system.

---

[4] See the discussion of bibliography cards, p. 134.

The Dewey Decimal system classifies all knowledge according to a numerical order from 000 (Generalities) to 900 (General Geography, History, and so forth), each class subdivided and sub-subdivided under that number, always using three whole numbers and possible additional decimals—for example, 228.195. The more numbers after the decimal, the narrower and more specialized the category into which the book fits. The letters and numbers of the second line of a Dewey Decimal call number indicate the author and the title. Be sure to include all of these on your bibliography card.

The Library of Congress system classifies fields of knowledge first under letters of the alphabet and then under numbers. The line of the call number following the period identifies the author and title.

It is not necessary to know the details of these classification systems; the order of arrangement in the stacks follows the line-by-line order in the call number system. With a very little practice, it is easy to move from one classification system to the other.

If you do not find the book you want on the shelf in its proper classified place, do not leave the stack tier without first looking in two other places. You may have forgotten to note "oversize" on your bibliography card. Check the oversize shelves which are usually at one end of the stack tier where books are classified according to call number within the oversize category. A second possibility is that the book has been checked out and returned but not yet reshelved. Check the reshelving carts and shelves which are usually near the elevator.

Using the stacks for research.   Not only do the stacks locate the book or books you know you want, they can also be a research resource. Once you have found the call numbers of several books in your subject of interest, you can go to the stacks and browse around in these call number areas. Usually you will turn up other books on your topic which may well prove to be more valuable than those you took from the subject file. Furthermore, with a bit of practice, you can quickly flip through a book in the stacks and ascertain whether it is worth reviewing in greater detail. This procedure saves a lot of research time and often turns up information which you would not otherwise find.

Reading in the stacks. Modern libraries often have their nicest reading areas in the stacks, complete with study desks and duplicating machines. In older, formerly closed-stack libraries, the reading facilities may be poor. If the environment is pleasant, reading in the stacks is much better than trying to work in a main reading room. You are closer to the books you need, and the area is usually much quieter and less distracting. When you finish your work in the stacks, leave your books on the table or reshelve shelves unless you see a sign asking you to reshelve them; most libraries prefer to have trained personnel reshelve the books. It cuts down on misplacement.

Circulation Desk

Here is where you sign out books that you want to take home or leave at a study desk or carrel. You will need to have a library or ID card which the college or university will issue to you, according to some special procedure, once you have paid your tuition and fees. You cannot take books out without your ID, but you can usually use books within the library.

Libraries invariably have a limit on the length of time a book can be kept out. This is usually two to four weeks (unless the book is on reserve). Normally, it is possible to renew a book once unless some other library user has placed a "hold" on it. It is important to return books on time because, if you do not, you will be fined. If fines accumulate, you will be forbidden to take books out of the library. If you have not paid outstanding fines at the beginning of a semester, you may be refused permission to register for courses. If you have outstanding fines at the end of your senior year, you may not be permitted to get your college diploma until they are paid. Furthermore, it is very inconsiderate to other users not to return books on time.

If the book or books you want are not on the shelves in the stacks, you can find out at the circulation desk where they are. Usually, somewhere near the desk will be a file of cards for books which have been temporarily removed to the reserve room. They may be filed in the usual fashion (author, title) or according to call number. These you will find in the reserve room, but you can use them only under reserve-room conditions. If you wait until the end of the semester, they will probably be returned to the regular stacks.

Books that are not on their regular shelves and not on reserve will usually be checked out to another user. You can request that a "hold" be placed on a book that you want. You will be informed when it is returned, and the book will be held for you at the circulation desk for a specified period of time.

Occasionally, a book will be at the bindery or lost. "At the bindery" means that it will be out for several weeks for rebinding. If it is lost, you can request that the book be "searched." When and if it is found, you will be informed. Since "at the bindery" and "lost" often mean a considerable wait or that the book may not turn up at all, it is wise to try another library. You can use the books of any open-stack library in the area.

If a book is not available simply because it has been lost or never bought, you can request your library to borrow it on inter-library loan. Find out how to do this from the circulation or reference librarian. The fact that this takes anywhere from a few days to a week or more is a good reason to start all research promptly.

The Reserve Room

Books and articles that are required reading for courses are often placed "on reserve," usually under the name and number of the course. Most libraries have two kinds of reserve—open and closed. If a book is on open reserve, you can take it out for two or three days. If it is on closed reserve, you must use it in the library, although, at some libraries, it can be taken out late in the day for overnight use and returned early on the morning of the next school day. Usually, all reserved books must be signed for, even those used in the library Reserve Room.

The Reference Room

Libraries almost invariably have a special area or room where reference books are kept. Reference books are dictionaries, encyclopedias, atlases, almanacs, yearbooks, handbooks, directories and other fact-finding volumes, both general and specific to various fields of knowledge. Reference books can be used only in the Reference Room; they may not be signed out. The card for a book in the Reference Room will always have "Ref." above the call number.

Indexes, Bibliographies and Abstracts

One way in which a college library is much better than a high school library is in the number of indexes, bibliographies and abstracts available to the researcher.

Indexes.   Indexes list articles and sometimes books which have been published on various subject-matter topics. The most important indexes are published at biweekly, monthly or quarterly intervals. For the period covered, they list, under author, title and subject headings, all the articles published in the periodicals analyzed by the index. The *Readers' Guide to Periodical Literature,* for example, indexes more than 150 popular periodicals. At the end of each year, all of the biweekly indexes of the *Guide* are condensed (duplications from one issue to another are omitted, but nothing is left out) into a single hard-cover volume. So, if you want to know whether anything has been published on your topic in *Harper's Magazine, Science News, Publishers' Weekly* or any one of the other periodicals surveyed by *Readers' Guide,* look up your topic in that index for the time period which you are interested in covering. A very large number of general and specialized indexes are available. The W. W. Wilson Company, publisher of the *Readers' Guide,* has listed in its pamphlet, "How to Use the Readers Guide to Periodical Literature," twenty-three other indexes which it publishes, all using the same format for classifying and listing articles.

Bibliographies. Bibliographies are lists of books devoted to the subject or subjects covered in particular fields, sometimes extremely specialized. The most useful of these are annotated, that is, they explain briefly the coverage of each volume listed and evaluate its worth to the reader.

Abstracts. Abstracts give brief summaries of important articles in various fields. Each volume of an abstract has an index. Look up the article in the index and get the location in the volume of the abstract. Reading an article in abstract can often save you time by making it unnecessary to read the entire article to find out if it has material bearing on your topic.

Indexes and abstracts are usually located in a section of the library either in or near the reference room. Bibliographies are usually located in the reference room itself. Since all of these are books, they are, of course, to be found in the card file, but it is often easier to find the index or abstract you want by browsing around that area of the library than it is to go first to the card file. Bibliographies will be listed in the subject catalog under the subject to which they apply. When making a bibliography card for an article listed in an index, abstract or bibliography, be sure to write on the card the name of the source, for example, *Readers' Guide*, 1976, p. 26. This information will be needed if a copy of the article or book must be ordered for you from another library.

The Periodical Room

Somewhere not far from the indexes and abstracts will be a special room and stack space devoted to the college or university's collection of periodicals. There will doubtless be two kinds of guides to its contents, a line index listing alphabetically all the periodicals which the library has and a card file, also alphabetical according to name of the periodical, giving more detail about which issues of each periodical are available and where they are located. The card or cards for each publication will not have a call number; periodicals are shelved in the periodicals stacks alphabetically according to title.

At one time, it was customary to shelve current periodicals on open stacks in the periodical room. However, since many journals have been stolen or articles cut out, a large number of libraries now make periodicals available only across the periodical-room circulation desk, where they must be signed out by the user. Usually, also, periodicals cannot be taken out of the library.

If your library does not have a particular periodical which you need for your research, you can order it. You will receive a duplicated copy of the article (not the periodical volume itself).

The Microfilm-Microfiche Room

Because the storage problem for printed materials is increasingly difficult, some kinds of periodicals and other materials are stored on microfilm or microfiche. This is particularly true of newspapers which are originally printed on a highly perishable kind of paper. Each microfilm room has its own card catalog, but the materials are likely to be listed in other catalogs in the library, too.

To read microfilm or microfiche requires special machines. You will need to get a librarian or clerk to show you how to use them when you first try to read material in this form. Needless to say, microfilm and microfiche cannot be duplicated on the regular library duplicating machines. Most microfilm-microfiche rooms now have special duplicating equipment which can be used by depositing a coin. The duplicates will be big enough to read without the machines.

The Documents Room

The Documents Room is where you will find stacked all the United States government documents and, frequently, state and local government documents as well. The number of these is very large.[5] United States government publications are catalogued according to a special system, and there are a number of bibliographies and indexes which list them. Finding them is often very tricky; it is best to ask the documents librarian for help.

Special Collections

Any library which has been in existence for a time is likely to have some special collections. These are probably housed in a separate location in the library, especially if they are valuable. Information about special collections can be obtained from the librarians.

The Computer

The computer will soon replace the card catalog and, most likely, many of the present indexes. Already there are a number of computer index services available. Computer indexes are very speedy to use and save much research time, but they are expensive because the cost is on a computer time-use basis. Many schools do not make them available to the students free. Therefore, you should consult with a librarian experienced in working with the computer who will help you narrow down your topic to only that information which you really need.[6]

GETTING HELP FROM THE LIBRARIANS

This brief survey of college library facilities does not cover everything available in any library. It is designed to help you

---

[5] The United States government is the largest publisher in the United States and probably in the world.

[6] I am grateful to the library staff at Adelphi University for their explanation of the use of library computer services.

find your way around a little better than most students do, at least at the beginning.

The most valuable resource which a library offers, other than the collection itself, is the librarians. Whenever you are in doubt as to how to find materials for a paper or any other project, ask. Not only can librarians help you locate materials which you would otherwise not learn about, but they often suggest time-saving methods of finding things for yourself. Students seem to feel that it is demeaning to ask a question of a librarian. There is nothing to be ashamed of in not knowing everything there is to know about the use of the library. Even librarians don't know everything about a library; most librarians are specialists in particular library skills and in particular fields of knowledge. When in doubt, or even if you think you know, ask. The librarians are there to help you.

Index

Abilities
    tested by Scholastic Aptitude Test, 7
    suited to college selected, 10–11, 13
Abstract(s), 66, 134
Admission(s)
    and grades, 105
    application for, 108–111
    competition for, 8
    criteria (requirements), 10, 105–111
    decile rankings and, 5 fn.
    office, 105, 107, 108
    professional school, 18, 105 fn., 105–111
    tests, 5–7, 106–107
Advisor, 15–16, 55
American College Testing Program (ACT), 5–7
Appendix to book, 37–38
Apprentice program, 112–113
Article(s), 63
    cited, 65
    evaluation of, 65–66
    in Reserve Room, 132
Assignment(s)
    and semester hours, 19
    for skills courses, 41
    weekly, 17
    weekly list of, 21–22
Association of American Law Schools, 111

"Back-up" school, 111
Bibliography(ies), 63, 134
    card, 64–65

Book(s), 17–18, 32–47, 65, 126–133
Book store, 17–18
Boredom
    and concentration, 28–29
    in class, 53

Call number, 64, 127, 129, 133
Campus activities, 11, 108
Card(s)
    bibliography, 64–65
    concentration and use of, 28
    for note taking, 42–44, 46, 67–68
    for review, 82
    organizing to write from, 70
Card catalog (file), 60, 126–129
Career(s)
    advanced education and, 103
    and major, 13
    athletic, 11
    counseling, 13, 104
    grades and, 104
    job relation to, 112–113, 116–117, 119
    planning, 4–13, 102–105
    tests for interest, 7
Carrel, library, 126
Chairperson of department, 104–105, 108
Circulation desk, 131–132
Class(es)
    attendance, 3, 49–51, 55
    concepts emphasized in, 82

Class(es) *(cont.)*
  ranking (standing), 1, 5, 8
  regular (as distinguished from seminars),
    51–55
  seminar(s), 55–56
Classic, 44–45
College(s)
  book store, 17–18
  bulletin, 12, 15, 123
  class (i.e., freshman, etc.), 9, 12–13, 16,
    103, 116
  counselling office (service), 5, 13, 104,
    113
  course(s), 10, 14, 15–16, 17, 18, 39, 41,
    48
  graduate's advantages, 48, 114
  major, selection of, 12–13
  placement office (service), 104, 113–114
  records and further education, 104
  selection of, 9–12
  viewpoint on opinions, 81–82
College Entrance Examination Board, 6
Combined score, 6
Common knowledge, 70
Composite score, 6
Computer, 136
Concentration, 25, 26–31, 41
Conclusion, 61
Content courses, 39
Costs, 9–10, 49, 104
Counselling office (service), 5, 13, 104,
  113
Course load, 14, 15–16, 17
Cramming, 74 fn.
Credit, 13, 91

Decile, 5, 5 fn.
Dewey Decimal System, 130
Dictionary(ies), 71, 121–122, 133
Discussions in class, 52–54
Discipline (academic), 26 fn., 63
Documents Room, 126 fn., 127, 135–
  136
Drafts (of research paper), 70–71
Drop/Add, 17–18
Drugs (includes alcohol, tobacco), 27, 83
Duplicating
  machine for taking notes, 67
  machine printout, 70
  papers, 72
  old examinations, 81

Education
  attitudes toward, 103
  whether to seek advanced, 3, 103–104
  time required for, 8
Educational Testing Service (ETS), 106–
  107, 109–111
Edwards Personal Preference Schedule, 7
Ellipsis(ses), 68
Employers, 118, 119
Employment (job)
  after graduation, 103
  and good grades, 1–2
  and tests, 1–2
  before graduation, 112–113
  getting a, 114–120
  market, 48, 113
  meaning of "decent," 111
  relation to career, 112–114, 119
Encyclopedia(s), 63, 65, 133
Endnotes, 70
Entrance to college, 5–10
Essay examination (test), 76–83, 90–
  100
Evaluation of teachers, 15
Evidence
  filling gaps in, 69
  place in outlines, 69
  place in research papers, 61–62
Examination(s) (see also tests)
  assignments covered by, 81
  civil service, 115–116
  finals week for, 14
  "fudging" on, 95
  grading (scoring), 6, 77–80
  importance of grades on, 3
  objective (short answer), 75–76, 81–82,
    85–90
  outlining in, 92–94, 96–98
  resting before, 83
  studying for, 3, 74–81
  subjective (essay), 76–77, 82–83, 90–100
  take-home, 77
  taking, 84–100
  timing, 80

Federal Job Information Center, 116
Financial aid, 10–11, 23, 105
Footnote(s)
  references in books, 63
  use of, 70, 71 fn.
"Fudging," 95

Glossary, 70
Good grades
 and class attendance, 49–51
 and Drop/Add, 17
 and intelligence, 2
 and Pass/Fail, 17, 18
 importance of, 1–2
Government documents, 66
Grade(s)
 and career, 104
 and class attendance, 49–51
 and course of study, 2
 and incompletes, 19
 and papers, 3
 and self esteem, 2
 and the right college, 2
 average, 80 fn.
 in seminars, 55
 indicating academic accomplishment,
  105
 on examinations, 3, 79
Grade Point Average (GPA), 8, 16–21, 27,
  107, 110–111
Grading of examinations, 77–80
Graduate Record Examination (GRE), 106
Graduate school, 103
 admission, 1, 105, 105 fn.
 costs, 9
Graduation
 semester hours for, 14
 after, 103–105
 requirements, 123
Grammar book, 71, 71 fn., 122
Graphs, 35–36
Guessing, 89–90
Guidance counselor, 5

Habit(s), 2
Health, 26–27
High school record(s), 5, 8
Honors, 116

Incompletes, 19
Index
 in a book, 38
 line, 134
 to periodicals, 63, 133–134
Inference, 85–87
Information (see also knowledge)
 about careers, 102
 about courses and teachers, 15–16
 about curricula and schools, 4, 111

Information (cont.)
 about yourself, 4–5
 finding for a paper, 63–65
 "fudging," 95
 gaps in papers, 69
 to answer test questions, 85
Intelligence, 2
 and concentration, 27–28
 tests, 2, 5
Intelligence quotient (IQ), 2
Interviews, 109, 118–119

Job (see employment)
Journals, 65–66

Kinetic sense, 28, 28 fn.
Knowledge (see also information)
 about courses and teachers, 15–16, 49–
  50
 about yourself, 4–5
 common, 70
 from class attendance, 50–51
 on objective examinations, 81
Kuder Preference Record, 7

Law degree, time required for, 8
Law School Admission Council, 111
Law School Admission Test (LSAT), 106,
  111
Learning
 about examinations, 75
 and health, 26–27
 as pleasure and as work, 3
 in content courses, 39–41
 in skills courses, 41–44
 memorization in, 42–44
 repetition in, 74
Lecture
 as source of research topic, 59
 notes, 52
 too difficult, 53
Librarian, 104, 105, 115, 136–137
 reference, 60, 63
Library, 27, 125–137
 as source of information on jobs, 114
 book not available in, 64
 call number, 64
 card catalog (file), 60, 63
 preliminary research in, 60
 public, 8 fn.
Library of Congress System, 130
"Lifting," 57–58

Loans
    instead of paid work, 23
    interest on, 9–10
    weight of, 104

Major
    and Pass/Fail, 19
    changing, 24
    requirements, 13
    selection of, 12–13
Master's degree, 103–104
Math score on SAT, 10
Media, definition of, 59 fn.
Medical degree, time required for, 8
Memorization, 24, 26, 42
Microfilm-microfiche Room, 135
Minority status, 105, 105 fn., 111
Motivation, 21–22, 24

Non-classic, 45–46
Non-conscious mind, 30
    definition, 30 fn.
Note taking, 27
    from content-course textbooks, 40–41
    from skills-course textbooks, 41–44
    from outside readings, 46–47
    for research, 67–69
    in class, 52
    on 3 x 5 cards, 42–44, 46, 67–68
Notes (foot- and end-), 36–37, 63, 70

Objective examination(s) (tests), 75–76, 78,
        81–82, 85–90
Opinions
    authors', 81
    college viewpoint on, 81–82
    friends', 5
    quotation of, 70
    students', 15
    teachers', 81–82
Outline
    expanding, 69
    form for notes, 40–41
    of essay answers, 92–94, 96–98
    of letter of application, 108
    preliminary, 61–63
Outside readings, 44–47

Pamphlets, 66
Paraphrasing, 67–68
Parents, 7

Paper(s) (see also research papers)
    and grades, 3
    as part of work load, 17, 19
    drafts of, 70–71
    length of, 59, 59 fn.
    parts of, 61–62
    readability, 70
    writing as a skill, 3
Pass/Fail, 17, 18
Percentile rank, 6
Periodical Room, 134–135
Personal file, 122–123
Personal qualities, 108–109
Placement office (service), 104, 113–114
Plagiarism, 58
Planning
    a major, 12–13
    advantages of, 22
    and selection of the right college, 2, 4,
        9–12
    and selection of the right courses, 2, 16
    and self-knowledge, 4
    and self-motivation, 3, 20
    by listing tasks, 19–22
    for a career, 4, 7–9
    key to success, 4
    to balance work load, 3
    to keep up GPA, 2, 16
    to keep working, 21–22
    use of study time, 24–26, 73
Point of view in research papers, 59–60
Prelaw Handbook, 111
Professional school
    admission, 18, 105, 105 fn.
    costs, 9–10, 104
    success in, 1
    where to apply for, 109–111
Professions, 7–8
Professor, 15, 19

Quarter, 14
Question(s)
    about research topics, 60
    essay (subjective), 76–77, 82–83, 90–100
    in class, 51, 52, 53–55, 56
    objective, 75–76, 85–90
    "prepared," 77
    scoring on examinations, 78–79
Quitting school, 24
Quota, minority, 105 fn.
Quotation(s), 68–69, 70

Readers' Guide to Periodical Literature, 133
Reading, 3
  advantages of good, 47–48
  as a skill, 32, 120
  classics, 44–45
  completing as a reward, 25
  examination questions, 85, 87, 90
  for college courses, 32–48
  for research, 66
  improving, 47
  in the library, 125–126, 131
  load of courses, 17, 20
  "outside," 17, 20, 44–47
  problems and self-assessment, 4
  test instructions, 84
  to remember, 3, 32, 38–48
  variations in ability to, 19
"Real world," fear of, 103
Recommendations, letter(s) of, 108
Reference(s), 64–65
  books, 133
  librarian, 63
  notes, 37
  Room, 133
Regents of the University of California v. Allan Bakke (1977), 105 fn.
Registration, 16, 18
Regular class, 51–52
Remember(ing), 39–47, 51, 54
Reports
  in personal file, 123
  seminar, 55–56
Requirement(s)
  admission, 8, 10, 105–109
  and Pass/Fail, 19
  and withdrawal from a course, 18
  course, 55
  for advanced degrees, 8
  for major, 13
Research, 57–73
  as job-related skill, 120
  in card file (catalog), 63, 126–129
  in stacks, 130–131
  needed for papers, 57
  non-library, 61 fn.
  note taking for, 67–69
  queries about in seminars, 55–56
  reading for, 66
  sources, 63
Research papers (see also papers, research), 57–73

Reserve Room, 132–133
Resumé, 116–118
Roommate, 27
Reviewing, 39, 74–83
  graded examinations, 100–101

Scholarship, 10–11, 23
Scholastic Aptitude Test (SAT), 5–7, 10
Scholastic average, 8
School(s)
  admission requirements, 1, 10, 105–109, 105 fn.
  bulletin, 12, 15, 123
  costs, 9–10
  feelings about, 103
  graduate or professional, 1, 103, 105–111, 105 fn.
  quality of programs in, 10
  quitting, 24
  selection of, 9–12
Score(s)
  composite and combined, 6
  civil service examination, 116
  entitlement to, 5 fn.
Scoring examinations, 78–80
Self-assessment, 4–5
Self-discipline, 8–9
Semester
  as segment of school year, 14
  hour, 14, 19
  planning course load for, 15–16
  study load per, 14, 19–20
Seminar, 51, 55–56
Sex and choice of college, 11–12
Skill(s)
  concentration as a, 27–30
  emphasized on examinations, 81
  getting good grades as a, 2
  needed for graduate admission, 106
  needed for answering test questions, 85–100
  study, 103
Skills course, 41
Skimming, 66
Sources, 63, 65–66
Special collections, 127, 136
Specialization, time required for, 8
Speed reading courses, 48
Stack(s), 64, 125–126, 129–131
  closed, 125 fn.
  open, 125 fn.
Strong-Campbell Interest Inventory, 7

Student(s)
    as sources of information, 15, 53
    course load, 16
    evaluation of teachers, 15
    getting to know, 50
    reviewing with, 82
    self-assessment, 4–5
    tools, of, 121–124
Study
    faults, 23–26
    for examinations, 74–83
    habits and practice, 3
    learning to, 2
    making rewarding, 25, 31
    planning for, 16–22
    time, using effectively, 23–31
Syllabus, 17, 17 fn.

Tables, 35, 36
Teacher(s)
    and motivation, 20
    as source of research information, 63
    assigning research topics, 58
    assignments, 19
    boring, 53
    comments, 5
    evaluations, 15
    fairness, 49
    grading practices, 19, 58, 77–80
    information on, 15
    of humanities, 70
    office hours, 55
    prejudices, 49–50
    styles, 51–53
    when you don't understand, 53–55
Test(s) (see also examinations)
    achievement, 6
    admissions, 5–7, 106–107
    aptitude, 57, 106–107
    instructions, 84
    intelligence, 2, 5
    multiple-choice, 75–76
    scores, 5–6, 5 fn.
    specialized types, 77
    true-false, 75
    vocational preference, 7, 113
Test of Standard Written English (TSWE),
    5–6

Textbook(s)
    buying and exchanging, 17–18
    clarification of, 52
    for content course, 39–41
    for skills course, 41–44
    remembering content of, 38–47
    structure, 32–38
    tables and illustrations in, 35–37
    too difficult, 17–18
Thesaurus, 71, 71 fn.
Time
    use of, 24–26
    schedule for writing papers, 72–73
Topic(s)
    finding in an index, 66
    for test answer, 96–97
    picking to write about, 58–60
    sentence, 34
    statement and outline, 61–63
    writing about, 60–73
Transfer credit and evaluation, 13
Transcript, 20
Trimester, 14
Two-year college (junior college), 9, 10
Tuition, 9
    as part of school budget, 16
    cost per credit, 49
    parents paying, 7, 49
Typewriter, 124

United States Office of Personnel Manage-
    ment, 116
University(ies), 10 fn., 11, 108

Verbatim notes, 67–69
Vocational preference tests, 7, 113

Weaknesses and self-assessment, 4, 15–16,
    113
Withdrawal(s), 18, 55
Workload, 3, 15–22
Writing
    distaste for, 5
    essay answers, 90–100
    research papers, 57–73

Yourself, 4–5

DATE DUE

DEC 22 '82		
MAY 20 '87		
NOV 2 9 2007		